ASTD Training Basics Series

D0479851

RETURN ON INVESTMENT (ROI) *Basics*

PATRICIA PULLIAM PHILLIPS
JACK J. PHILLIPS

A Complete, How-to Guide to Help You:

 Understand and Apply Basic Principles and Practices

 Select Appropriate Programs to Measure

 Communicate Results and Sustain Momentum

ASTD Press

ASTD Press is an internationally renowned source of insightful and practical information on workplace learning and performance topics, including training basics, evaluation and return-on-investment (ROI), instructional systems development (ISD), e-learning, leadership, and career development.

Ordering information: Books published by ASTD Press can be purchased by visiting our Website at store.astd.org or by calling 800.628.2783 or 703.683.8100.

Library of Congress Control Number: 2004116270

ISBN: 1-56286-406-8

Acquisitions and Development Editor: Mark Morrow
Copyeditor: April Davis
Interior Design and Production: Kathleen Schaner
Cover Design: Renita Wade
Cover Illustration: Bek Shaklrov

Printed by Victor Graphics, Inc., Baltimore, Maryland, www.victorgraphics.com.

Table of Contents

About the
Training Basics Series

ASTD's *Training Basics* series recognizes and, in some ways, celebrates the fast-paced, ever-changing reality of organizations today. Jobs, roles, and expectations change quickly. One day you might be a network administrator or a process line manager, and the next day you might be asked to train 50 employees in basic computer skills or to instruct line workers in quality processes.

Where do you turn for help? The ASTD *Training Basics* series is designed to be your one-stop solution. The series takes a minimalist approach to your learning curve dilemma and presents only the information you need to be successful. Each book in the series guides you through key aspects of training: giving presentations, making the transition to the role of trainer, designing and delivering training, and evaluating training. The books in the series also include some advanced skills such as performance and basic business proficiencies.

The ASTD *Training Basics* series is the perfect tool for training and performance professionals looking for easy-to-understand materials that will prepare non-trainers to take on a training role. In addition, this series is the perfect reference tool for any trainer's bookshelf and a quick way to hone your existing skills. The titles currently planned for the series include:

- ▶ *Presentation Basics* (2003)
- ▶ *Trainer Basics* (2003)
- ▶ *Training Design Basics* (2003)
- ▶ *Facilitation Basics* (2004)
- ▶ *Communication Basics* (2004)
- ▶ *Performance Basics* (2004)
- ▶ *Evaluation Basics* (2005)
- ▶ *Needs Assessment Basics* (2005)
- ▶ *Return on Investment (ROI) Basics* (2005)
- ▶ *Organization Development Basics* (2005).

Preface

■■

Consider your most important program—one that is strategic, expensive, and high profile and attracts management attention. Suppose you decide to evaluate the success of the program. Through your analysis you find that participants:

- ▶ viewed the program as relevant to their work
- ▶ acquired new knowledge and skills
- ▶ used the knowledge and skills routinely on the job, although they had some difficulty in a few areas
- ▶ improved several important work unit measures, including quality and productivity
- ▶ achieved a 105% return on the investment in the program
- ▶ reported an increase in job satisfaction in their work unit.

To an audience reviewing the data, several questions surface. Who and what are the sources of the data? What assumptions are made in the analysis? Is the process consistent from one study to another? Is the study credible? What did it cost to produce the study?

From the program owner's perspective, other questions surface. What would this data mean for your program? What would it mean for your team and you personally? If the above results were negative, what would it mean for the program, your team, and you? How should the results be used?

These are the questions faced by hundreds who are beginning their journey into enhanced workplace learning and performance accountability. These are fundamental and universal questions. This book, *Return on Investment (ROI) Basics*, will help you answer these questions and understand the true meaning of return on investment (ROI).

What's Inside?

Each chapter provides the fundamental steps in developing a comprehensive evaluation. Although attempts have been made to address some of the more difficult issues, readers will become most comfortable with the basic techniques. By the end of the book, you will have basic skills in ROI, be able to select appropriate programs for ROI evaluation, and be able to develop a strategy to integrate ROI as part of your ongoing learning process.

Chapter 1, The Basics, provides an overview of ROI—what it means, how it is reported, and when it should be used.

Chapter 2, Plan Your Work, focuses on the most fundamental step of all—developing the measures that define program success.

Chapter 3, Collect Data, focuses on collecting the follow-up data. This chapter answers the questions: How do you collect data? From whom do you collect data? When do you collect data?

Chapter 4, Isolate Program Impact, addresses one of the most important steps in program evaluation. This step in the process answers the basic question: How do you know it was your program that improved these measures?

Chapter 5, Do the Math, presents the fundamental difference between reporting effects and reporting ROI. It's in the math. Only by converting impact measures to monetary value and comparing that value to the fully loaded cost of the program can an actual ROI be reported.

Chapter 6, Toot Your Horn, focuses on communicating results. Without communication, your evaluation efforts are in vain.

Chapter 7, Sustain Momentum, builds on the previous chapter. Anyone can conduct an ROI study, but can you integrate the process into the workplace learning and performance (WLP) process so that it is seamless and still effective?

The book is presented in a way that will make it easy for you to understand and apply what is learned. Icons help identify key points.

What's Inside This Chapter

Each chapter opens with a short list to introduce you to the chapter. This section contains the three basic lessons to be learned.

Think About This

These considerations attempt to present the information in a slightly different way to reinforce learning as well as to generate the "aha moment" that may not have occurred earlier in the chapter.

Basic Rules

These rules present guiding principles and rules of thumb to ensure consistent application of the ROI methodology presented in the book.

Noted

The noted icon presents a point or issue that needs to be highlighted.

Getting It Done

This final section of each chapter contains a challenge or action item to set the process in motion.

Who Should Read This Book?

The book is targeted to beginners who have been challenged to implement a comprehensive evaluation process as well as those who are taking a proactive approach to accountability. However, those who are more advanced, but still question key issues, will find value in reading this book. Workplace learning and performance managers will also benefit from reading this book. By understanding the basics, managers can better serve as champions for ROI implementation.

What Do We Mean?

Before delving into the material, a few definitions may be helpful. *Program*, refers to the initiative being evaluated. This could be a course, a full-scale change initiative, or a learning management system implementation. *Workplace learning and performance* refers to training, performance improvement, learning, development, and education. The *levels of evaluation* refer to the levels defined in the five-level ROI framework. *ROI* is defined in the true sense of the acronym—earnings divided by investment or net benefits divided by costs.

We hope this book will help you as you move forward with ROI. Best of luck to all of you who do!

Acknowledgments

A book cannot be written without thanking those who make it happen. First, thanks to ASTD for giving us another opportunity to contribute to the industry knowledge bank. We believe in the methodology presented here and have observed its successful application in organizations throughout the world. We appreciate ASTD's recognition of its importance. Special thanks go to Mark Morrow for his patience and persistence as he continues to support us in our publishing efforts with ASTD.

Thanks go to Joyce Alff. She has jumped through one more hoop to help us produce another publication. We thank you, Joyce, more than we can say. Also, thanks go to our staff, Ashley Horton, Margaret Marston, and Francine Hawkins, who continue to support us and cheer us on.

We'd also like to thank our many workshop participants. Without you, we would have few stories to tell and limited ways in which we could tell them. We appreciate your candor and help in addressing the many issues faced by WLP professionals pursuing this challenging topic.

Jack and Patti Phillips
December 2005

1

The Basics

What's Inside This Chapter

This chapter explores the fundamentals of the return on investment (ROI) methodology, which is presented in this book. The fundamentals cover three key issues:

▶ Defining ROI
▶ Getting there
▶ Using it.

Defining ROI

So what is ROI? ROI is the ultimate measure of accountability that answers the question: Is there a financial return for investing in a program, process, initiative, or performance improvement solution? It is an economic indicator—meaning, you are dealing with math. The concept of comparing earnings to investment has been used in business for centuries to measure the success of a variety of investment opportunities. It is becoming common practice in organizational functions that are viewed as cost centers, including workplace learning and performance (WLP).

ROI's counterpart, benefit-cost analysis, is grounded in welfare economics. As far back as 1667 in London, Sir William Petty found that public health expenditures to combat the plague would achieve what is now referred to as a benefit-cost ratio

(BCR) of 84 to 1 (84:1). Benefit-cost analysis became prominent in the United States in the early 1900s when it was used to justify projects initiated under the River and Harbor Act of 1902 and the Flood Control Act of 1936. ROI and the benefit-cost ratio provide similar indicators of investment success, though one (ROI) presents the earnings (net benefits) as compared to the cost, while the other (BCR) compares benefits to costs. Below are the basic equations used to calculate the benefit-cost ratio and the ROI:

$$BCR = \text{Program Benefits} \div \text{Program Costs}$$

$$ROI\ (\%) = (\text{Net Program Benefits} \div \text{Program Costs}) \times 100$$

What do these equations mean? A benefit-cost ratio of 2:1 means that for every $1 invested, you get $2 back. This translates into an ROI of 100%, which says that for every $1 invested, you get $1 back after the costs are covered (you get your investment back plus $1).

Benefit-cost ratios were used in the past primarily in public sector settings, while ROI was used primarily by accountants managing funds in business and industry. Either can be, and are, used in both settings, but it is important to understand the difference. In many cases the benefit-cost ratio and the ROI are reported together.

Noted

Periodically, someone will report a benefit-cost ratio of 3:1, for example, and an ROI of 300%. This is incorrect. ROI is the net benefits divided by the costs, which translates to 200%. The net benefit is equal to benefits minus costs.

Though ROI is the ultimate measure of profitability, basic accounting practice says that reporting the ROI metric alone is insufficient. To be truly meaningful, ROI must be reported with other performance measures.

ROI and the Levels of Evaluation

ROI for WLP is reported in the context of the five-level ROI framework. These levels represent categories of data:

Think About This

A shortcut to calculate the ROI from a benefit-cost ratio is to subtract 1 from the benefit-cost ratio. For instance, a benefit-cost ratio of 5.25:1 tells you that for every $1 you invest, you get $5.25 back. By subtracting 1 from 5.25 (5.25 − 1.00 = 4.25) and multiplying the difference by 100, you get an ROI of 425%. (For every $1 you invest, you get back $4.25 after costs.)

▶ Level 1 *Reaction, Satisfaction, and Planned Action*—Data representing participants' reactions to the program and their planned actions is collected and analyzed. Reactions may include participants' views of the course content, facilitation, and learning environment. This category of data also includes data often used to predict application of acquired knowledge and skills, including relevance, importance, amount of new information, and participants' willingness to recommend the program to others.

▶ Level 2 *Learning*—Data representing the extent to which participants acquired new knowledge and skills is collected and analyzed. This category of data also includes the level of confidence participants have in their ability to apply what they have learned.

▶ Level 3 *Application and Implementation*—Data is collected and analyzed to determine the extent to which participants effectively apply their newly acquired knowledge and skills. This category also includes data that describes the barriers that prevent application and any supporting elements (enablers) in the knowledge transfer process.

▶ Level 4 *Business Impact*—Data is collected and analyzed to determine the extent to which participants' applications of acquired knowledge and skills positively influenced key measures that were intended to improve as a result of the program. When reporting data at Level 4, a step to isolate the program's effects on these measures from other influences is always taken.

▶ Level 5 *Return on Investment*—Impact measures are converted to monetary values and compared with the fully loaded program costs. You can have improvement in productivity, for example, but you must determine the monetary value of that improvement and what that improvement cost you in order to calculate ROI. If the monetary value of productivity's improvement exceeds the cost, your calculation results in a positive ROI.

Noted

The levels of evaluation are categories of data; timing of data collection does not necessarily define the level to which you are evaluating. Level 1 data can be collected in a follow-up evaluation months after the program, as well as at the end of the program when it is typically collected. Level 4 data can be estimated before a program is implemented or at the end of the program when a forecast is necessary, as well as collected after the program is implemented when actual improvement can be observed. The appendix provides an overview of this forecasting option.

Each level of evaluation answers basic questions regarding the program success. Table 1-1 presents these questions.

The reason for referring to evaluation data as levels is that it facilitates managing and reporting the data. More important, however, these five levels present data in a way that makes it easy for the audience to understand the results reported. Each level of evaluation provides important, stand-alone data. Reported together, the five-level ROI framework represents data that tells the complete story of program success or failure. Figure 1-1 presents the chain of impact that occurs as participants react positively to a program, acquire knowledge and skills, apply the knowledge and skills, and, as a consequence, positively affect key business measures. When these business measures are converted to monetary value and compared to the fully loaded costs, ROI is calculated. Along with the ROI and the four other categories of data, intangible benefits are reported. These represent Level 4 measures not converted to monetary value.

The five-level ROI framework is just one piece of an overall evaluation puzzle. Four additional puzzle pieces make up a comprehensive, sustainable evaluation practice.

Evaluation Puzzle

There are five pieces to the evaluation puzzle, as shown in figure 1-2. The evaluation framework previously described is the first piece, providing a way to categorize and report data.

Table 1-1. Evaluation framework and key questions.

Level of Evaluation	Key Questions
Level 1: Reaction, Satisfaction, and Planned Action	• Was the program relevant to participants' jobs and mission? • Was the program important to participants' jobs and mission success? • Did the program provide new information? • Do participants intend to use what they learned? • Would participants recommend the program to others? • Is there room for improvement with facilitation, materials, and the learning environment?
Level 2: Learning	• Did participants acquire the knowledge and skills presented in the program? • Do participants know how to apply what they learned? • Are participants confident to apply what they learned?
Level 3: Application and Implementation	• How effective are participants at applying what they learned? • How frequently are participants applying what they learned? • If participants are applying what they learned, what is supporting them? • If participants are not applying what they learned, why not?
Level 4: Business Impact	• So what if the application is successful? • To what extent did application of learning improve the measures the program was intended to improve? • How did the program affect output, quality, cost, time, customer satisfaction, employee satisfaction, and other measures? • How do you know it was the program that improved these measures?
Level 5: ROI	• Do the monetary benefits of the improvement in business impact measures outweigh the cost of the program?

Source: The ROI Institute.

ROI Process Model. The second piece of the puzzle includes a process model. The process model serves as a step-by-step guide to help maintain a consistent approach to evaluation. There are four phases to the process, each containing critical steps that must be taken to get to credible information. These four phases are described in more detail later in this chapter:

1. Evaluation planning
   a. Develop/review objectives
   b. Develop evaluation plans and baseline data
2. Data collection
   a. Collect data during the program
   b. Collect data after the program

Figure 1-1. Chain of impact.

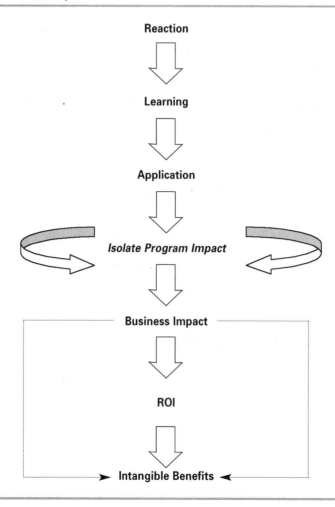

3. Data analysis
   a. Isolate the effects of the program
   b. Convert data to monetary value
   c. Tabulate program costs
   d. Identify intangible benefits
   e. Calculate the ROI
4. Reporting
   a. Develop impact study
   b. Communicate results to stakeholders.

Think About This

Consider the chain of impact in Figure 1-1:

- Can participants react positively and still not acquire knowledge and skills?
- Can participants acquire knowledge and skills and not apply them?
- Can participants apply knowledge and skills and still observe no positive impact on business measures?
- Can positive impact still result in a negative ROI?

If you answered *yes*, you are correct. Each category of data is independent with the exception of Level 5, which depends on Level 4 measures to start the benefit-cost comparison process. But, if you have a negative or extremely high ROI and you have not collected and analyzed data at the lower levels, how do you explain the results?

By reporting data at all levels, you have the information you need to explain why you achieved the results and how you can improve them in the future.

Figure 1-2. Evaluation puzzle.

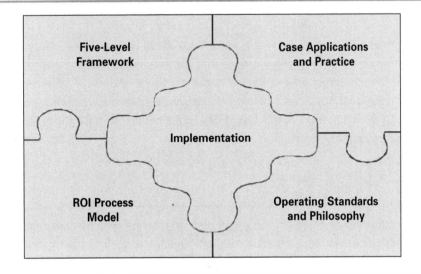

Source: Phillips, J.J. (2000). *The Consultants Scorecard: Tracking Results and Bottom Line Impact of Consulting Projects.* New York: McGraw-Hill.

Noted

The ROI methodology presented in this book is a much updated and revised approach to Kirkpatrick's evaluation levels. Here are the basic differences between the Kirkpatrick four-level framework and the ROI methodology presented in this book:

1. *Level 3—Kirkpatrick refers to job behavior; this book refers to application and implementation, which can include more than behavior change. Although behavior is inherently a part of all activity, sometimes the focus of applied knowledge and skills considers more than behavior change.*

2. *Level 4—Kirkpatrick refers to results; this book refers to business impact, which is the consequence of the application of knowledge gained. This book considers all levels of evaluation to be results versus activity. Level 4 represents the impact of achieving successful results at each previous level.*

3. *Isolating Program Impact—Kirkpatrick doesn't require it; this approach does. Many researchers suggest this can only be done using a control group. All agree that a control group is not always feasible. This book's approach requires the step be taken, even if by other techniques, rather than ignoring the issue. This book argues that without this step, a study is invalid.*

4. *Level 5—Kirkpatrick includes ROI at Level 4; this book identifies it as a separate level because new data and additional steps are necessary to move from Level 4 to Level 5. A comprehensive evaluation can stop at Level 4, excluding the cost of the program. It is possible for success to be realized at Level 4 (the program has influenced a business impact measure), yet the program can have a negative ROI value because of excessive costs, hence, the need for ROI. Level 5 provides this ultimate economic measure of program success, but it does not discount the importance of intangible benefits—those measures not converted to monetary value.*

5. *This book's approach provides a systematic process for collecting, analyzing, and reporting data, including intangibles.*

6. *This book presents standards for using the process to ensure consistent application.*

7. *This book focuses on implementation of the process, recognizing that the best framework or model will be ineffective if it is not properly implemented.*

Think About This

Is your organization large with autonomous divisions? Many organizations pursuing ROI fit this description. Competition sometimes exists between divisions. This can lead to each division purposefully approaching evaluation (and many other things) differently from other divisions.

If each division approaches evaluation, including ROI, using different methodologies and different standards, doesn't it stand to reason that when results are compared there is no comparison?

Whether it is the approach presented in this book or some other approach, find one, develop it, use existing standards supporting the approach, and apply the approach consistently.

Operating Standards and Philosophy. This puzzle piece ensures consistent decision making around the application of the model. Standards provide the guidance needed to support the process and ensure consistent, reliable practice. By following the 12 principles shown in table 1-2, consistent results can be achieved. These guiding principles help maintain a conservative and credible approach to data collection and analysis. These 12 principles serve as decision-making tools, influencing decisions on the best approach by which to collect data, the best source and timing for data collection, the most appropriate approach for isolation and data conversion, the costs to be included, and the stakeholders to whom results are reported.

Case Applications and Practice. Applying the ROI methodology while adhering to the guiding principles is not a simple task. Case applications and practice, the fourth piece of the evaluation puzzle, provides a deeper understanding of this comprehensive evaluation process. Case application also provides evidence of program success—without the story, who will know? Thousands of case studies have been developed describing the application of the ROI methodology. These case studies represent work from business and industry, health care, government, and even community and faith-based initiatives.

Practitioners who are beginning their pursuit of ROI can learn from these case studies, as well as those found in other publications; however, the best learning

Table 1-2. Twelve guiding principles for effective ROI implementation.

1. When a higher level of evaluation is conducted, data must be collected at lower levels.
2. When an evaluation is planned for a higher level, the previous level of evaluation does not have to be comprehensive.
3. When collecting and analyzing data, use only the most credible source.
4. When analyzing data, choose the most conservative among alternatives.
5. At least one method must be used to isolate the effects of the solution/program.
6. If no improvement data is available for a population or from a specific source, it is assumed that little or no improvement has occurred.
7. Estimates of improvements should be adjusted (discounted) for the potential error of the estimate.
8. Extreme data items and unsupported claims should not be used in ROI calculations.
9. Only the first year of benefits should be used in the ROI analysis for short-term solutions/programs.
10. Costs of the solution/program should be fully loaded for ROI analysis.
11. Intangible measures are defined as measures that are purposely not converted to monetary value.
12. The results from the ROI methodology must be communicated to all key stakeholders.

Source: The ROI Institute.

comes from actual application. Conducting your own ROI study will allow you to see how the framework, process model, and operating standards come together. It also serves as a starting line for your track record of program success.

Implementation. Conducting just one study adds little value to your efforts to continuously improve and account for your workplace learning and performance programs. The key is implementation—the last and most critical piece of the evaluation puzzle. Anyone can conduct one ROI study; the key is sustaining the practice. Building the philosophy into everyday decisions about your WLP process is imperative if you want this (or any) comprehensive evaluation process to have longevity. This requires assessing your organization's culture for accountability; assessing your organization's readiness for ROI; defining the purpose for pursuing this level of evaluation; building expertise and capability; and creating tools, templates, and standard processes.

Getting There

To get to ROI, it is important to follow a step-by-step process to ensure consist, reliable results. Ten steps taken during four phases make up the process. Figure 1-3 presents the ROI model.

Figure 1-3. ROI methodology process model.

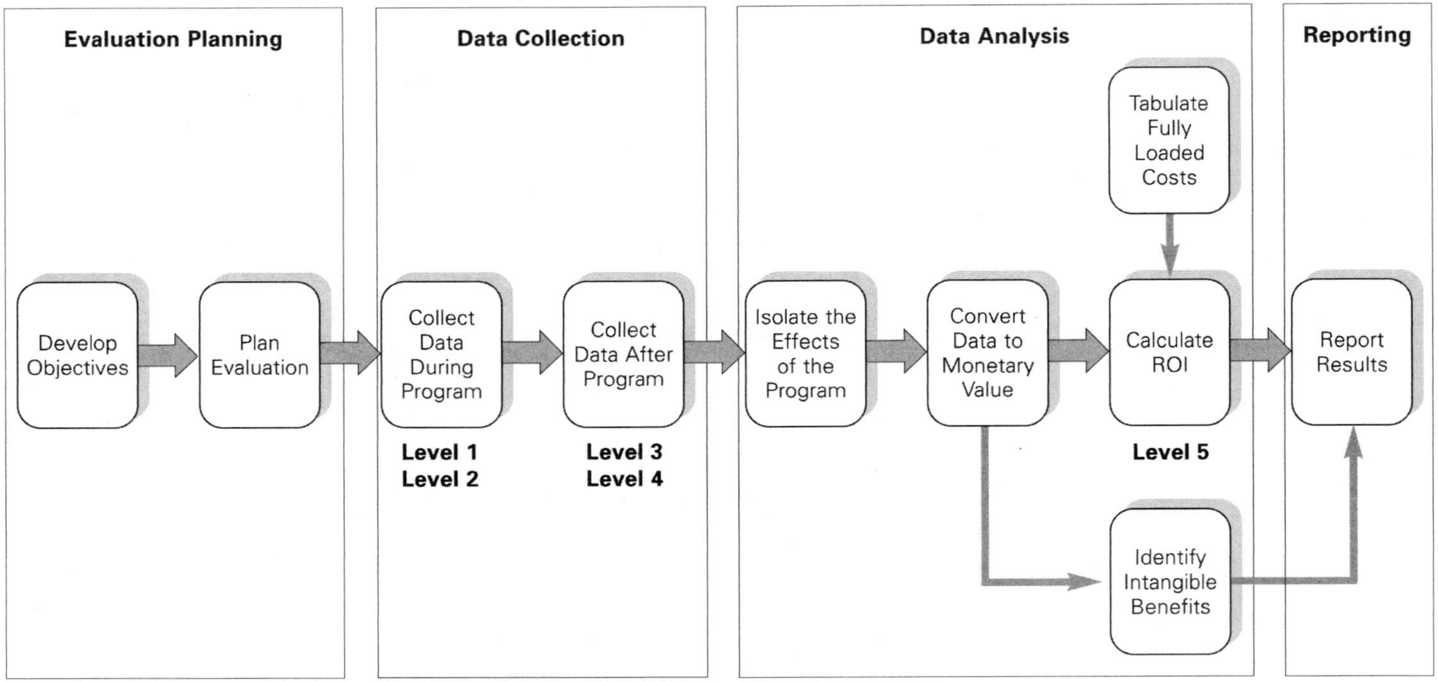

| Evaluation Planning | Data Collection | Data Analysis | Reporting |

Evaluation Planning
- Develop Objectives
- Plan Evaluation

Data Collection
- Collect Data During Program — Level 1 Level 2
- Collect Data After Program — Level 3 Level 4

Data Analysis
- Isolate the Effects of the Program
- Convert Data to Monetary Value
- Tabulate Fully Loaded Costs
- Calculate ROI — Level 5
- Identify Intangible Benefits

Reporting
- Report Results

Evaluation Planning

Planning your ROI evaluation is the first step in successful application. Without a plan it will be difficult for you to know where you are going, much less know when you arrive. Your plan begins with the development and review of the program objectives. From there you develop your data collection plan. This includes defining the measures for each level of evaluation, selecting the data collection instrument, identifying the source of the data, and timing of data collection. Any available baseline data for the measures you are taking should be collected during this time. Next, you develop the ROI analysis plan at which point you select the most appropriate technique to isolate the effects of the program on impact data and the most credible method for converting data to money. Cost categories and communication targets are developed.

Data Collection

Once the planning phase is completed, data collection begins. Collecting data is Step 1 in the execution of the plan. Levels 1 and 2 data is collected during the program with common instruments, including end-of-course questionnaires, written tests and exercises, demonstrations, and a variety of other techniques. Follow-up data, Levels 3 and 4, is collected sometime after the program when application of the newly acquired knowledge and skills becomes routine and when enough time has passed to observe impact on key measures.

Data Analysis

Once the data becomes available, analysis begins. But remember, during the planning stage you decided the best approach for analysis; so when the time comes, it's just a matter of execution. Isolating the effects of the program on impact data is a first step in data analysis. This step is taken when collecting data at Level 4. Often overlooked in evaluating success of workplace learning and performance programs, this step answers the critical question, "How do you know it was your program that improved the measures?"

The move from Level 4 to Level 5 begins with converting Level 4 impact measures to monetary value. Often this step instills the greatest fear in WLP professionals, but once you understand the available techniques to convert data along with the five-steps to do it, the fear usually subsides.

Fully loaded costs are developed during the data analysis phase. These costs include needs assessment (when conducted), design, delivery, and evaluation costs. The intent is to leave no cost stone unturned!

Intangible benefits are identified during this phase. These are the Level 4 measures not converted to monetary value. They can also represent any unplanned program benefits, which, of course, are not identified during the planning phase.

The last step of the data analysis phase is the math. Using simple addition, subtraction, multiplication, and division, the ROI is calculated.

Reporting

This is the most important phase in the evaluation process. Evaluation without communication is a worthless endeavor. If you tell no one how the program is progressing, how can you improve the WLP process, secure additional funding, justify programs, and market programs to future participants?

A variety of ways are available to report data. There are micro reports that include the complete ROI impact study; there are macro reports for all programs that include scorecards, dashboards, and other reporting tools.

Using It

The ultimate use of data generated through the ROI methodology is to show value of programs, specifically economic value. There are a variety of other uses for this data, including to justify spending, improve the WLP process, and gain support.

Justify Spending

Justification of spending is becoming more commonplace in the WLP practice than it was in the past. WLP managers are often required to justify investing in new programs, in the continuation of existing programs, and in changes or enhancements to existing programs.

New Programs. In the past, when the WLP practice had "deep pockets," new programs were brought on board every time a best seller hit the *New York Times*. While many programs were inspiring, there was no business justification for them. Today, new programs undergo a certain amount of scrutiny. At a minimum, WLP managers consider the costs and provide some esoteric justification for investing the resources.

For those who are serious about justifying investments in new programs, ROI is a valuable tool. ROI for new programs can be forecasted using a variety of techniques; but for new programs where a preprogram justification is required, there are two approaches: preprogram forecasts and ROI in pilot programs. Although these approaches are beyond the scope of this book, basic descriptions of the forecasting techniques are described in the appendix.

Existing Programs. Calculating ROI in existing programs is more common in practice than forecasting success for new programs, although there is an increased interest in program justification prior to launch. Typically, ROI is used to justify investments in existing programs. These are programs where development and delivery have taken place, but there is concern that the value does not justify continuing the program.

Along with justifying the continuation of existing programs, ROI is used to determine the value of changing delivery mechanisms, such as incorporating blended learning or placing a program online with no in-person interaction. It is also used to justify investing in additional support interventions that supplement the learning transfer process. Four approaches to ROI can assist in justifying the investment in existing programs: forecasting at Levels 1, 2, and 3 and the postprogram evaluation. Postprogram evaluation is the basis for this book.

Improve the WLP Process

The most important use of ROI is to improve the WLP process. Often WLP staff and program participants are threatened by the thought of being evaluated to such an extent. However, program evaluation is about making decisions concerning the program and the process, not about the individual performance of the people involved in the program. ROI can improve the WLP process by helping staff to set priorities, eliminate unsuccessful programs, and reinvent the WLP function.

Set Priorities. In almost all organizations, the need for WLP exceeds the available resources. A comprehensive evaluation process, including ROI, can help determine which programs rank as the highest priority. Programs with greatest impact (or the potential for greatest impact) are often top priority. Of course, this approach has to be moderated by taking a long view, ensuring that developmental efforts are in place for a long-term payoff. Also, some programs are necessary and represent commitments by the organization. Those concerns aside, the programs generating the greatest impact or potential impact should be given the highest priority when allocating resources.

Eliminate Unsuccessful Programs. You hate to think of eliminating programs—to some people this translates into the elimination of responsibility, ultimately the

Think About This

WLP staff, participants, and participant supervisors know a vendor-supplied customer service program provides little value to the organization. Participants provided evidence of this with their comments on the end-of-course questionnaire. Unfortunately, Level 1 data is ignored by the leaders. They need stronger evidence that the program is ineffective.

With this edict, the evaluation team sets the course for implementing a comprehensive evaluation to provide the much needed data. The evaluation results show that in the first year, the program achieves a negative 85% ROI; the second year forecast shows a slightly less negative ROI of negative 54%. Immediately leaders agree to drop the program.

Sometimes you need to speak the language of business to get your point across.

elimination of jobs. This is not necessarily true. For years, the WLP function has had limited tools to eliminate what are known to be unsuccessful, unnecessary programs. ROI provides this tool.

Reinvent the WLP Function. Implementing a comprehensive evaluation process can have many long-term payoffs, one of which is the reinvention of the WLP process. While evaluating to the ROI level is not necessary for all programs, the process itself provides valuable data that can help eliminate unsuccessful programs or reinvent those that are successful but expensive. The funds saved by making these decisions can be transferred to the front-end assessment, resulting in better, more focused programs. This allows for better alignment between the WLP and the business and perpetuates long-term alignment.

Noted

Many people fear a negative ROI; however, more is learned through evaluation projects that achieve a negative ROI than those achieving a high, positive ROI.

Basic Rule 1

All programs should not be evaluated to Level 5. ROI is reserved for those programs that are expensive, have a broad reach, drive business impact, have the attention of senior managers, or are highly visible in the organization. However, when evaluation does go to Level 5, results should be reported at the lower levels to ensure that the complete story is told.

Gain Support

A third use for ROI is to gain support for programs and the WLP process. A successful WLP function needs support from key executives and administrators. Showing the ROI for programs can alter managers' and supervisors' perceptions and enhance the respect and credibility of the learning staff.

Key Executives and Administrators. Probably senior executives and administrators are the most important group to the WLP function; they commit resources and show support for functions achieving results that positively affect the strategy of the organization. Known for their support of learning, executives and administrators often suggest training as the solution to all problems. Unfortunately, training is not always the solution, so when the problem exists after training, executives and administrators quickly turn coats. That is why it is not uncommon to find WLP absent from the decision-making table.

To ensure WLP's seat at the table, it is necessary for the WLP staff and management to think like a business—focusing programs on results and organizational strategy. ROI is one way this focus can occur. WLP can easily position the function to be a strategic player in the organization by thinking through the opportunity or financial problem that needs to the solved; translating that into the business need; assessing the job performance that needs to be applied to meet the business need; determining the skills necessary to ensure successful job performance; and, finally, deciding the best approach to deliver the knowledge needed to build the skills. ROI evaluation provides the economic justification and value of investing in the mechanism selected to solve the problem.

Managers and Supervisors. Mid-level and first-level supervisors can sometimes be WLP's antagonists. They often question the value of training because they aren't interested in what their employees learn; rather, they are interested in what employees *do* with what they learn. WLP must take learning a step further by showing the effect of what employees do with what they learn with particular emphasis on measures representative of output, quality, cost, and time. If WLP programs can show results linked to the business and WLP staff can speak the language of business, mid-level managers and supervisors may start to listen to WLP more closely.

Employees. Showing the value of WLP programs, including ROI, can enhance the WLP function's overall credibility. By showing that the programs offered are serious programs achieving serious results, employees will view training as a valuable way to spend time away from their pressing duties. Also, by making adjustments in programs based on the evaluation findings, employees will see that the evaluation process is not just a superficial attempt to show value.

Getting It Done

It is easy to describe the basics and benefits of using such a comprehensive evaluation process as the ROI methodology, but this methodology is not for everyone. Given that, your first step toward making ROI work for your organization is assessing the degree to which your WLP function is results based. Complete the assessment in exercise 1-1 to see where you stand. Then ask a client to complete the survey and compare the results.

Exercise 1-1. WLP programs assessment.

Instructions: For each of the following statements, circle the response that best matches the WLP function at your organization.

1. The direction of the WLP function at your organization
    a) shifts with requests, problems, and changes as they occur.
    b) is determined by WLP and adjusted as needed.
    c) is based on a mission and a strategic plan for the function.

2. The primary mode of operation of the WLP function is
    a) to respond to requests by managers and other employees to deliver training services.
    b) to help management react to crisis situations and reach solutions through training services.
    c) to implement many WLP programs in collaboration with management to prevent problems and crisis situations.

3. The goals of the WLP function are
    a) set by the WLP staff based on perceived demand for programs.
    b) developed consistent with WLP plans and goals.
    c) developed to integrate with operating goals and strategic plans of the organization.

4. Most new programs are initiated
    a) by request of top management.
    b) when a program appears to be successful in another organization.
    c) after a needs analysis has indicated that the program is needed.

5. When a major organizational change is made
    a) you decide only which presentations are needed, not which skills are needed.
    b) you occasionally assess what new skills and knowledge are needed.
    c) you systematically evaluate what skills and knowledge are needed.

6. To define WLP plans
    a) management is asked to choose WLP programs from a list of canned, existing courses.
    b) employees are asked about their WLP needs.
    c) WLP needs are systematically derived from a thorough analysis of performance problems.

7. When determining the timing of training and the target audiences
    a) you have lengthy, nonspecific WLP training courses for large audiences.
    b) you tie specific WLP training needs to specific individuals and groups.
    c) you deliver WLP training almost immediately before its use, and it is given only to those people who need it.

8. The responsibility for results from WLP
    a) rests primarily with the WLP staff to ensure that the programs are successful.
    b) is the responsibility of the WLP staff and line managers, who jointly ensure that results are obtained.
    c) is a shared responsibility of the WLP staff, participants, and managers all working together to ensure success.

9. Systematic, objective evaluation, designed to ensure that participants are performing appropriately on the job
    a) is never accomplished. The only evaluations are during the program and they focus on how much the participants enjoyed the program.
    b) is occasionally accomplished. Participants are asked if the training was effective on the job.
    c) is frequently and systematically pursued. Performance is evaluated after training is completed.

10. New programs are developed
    a) internally, using a staff of instructional designers and specialists.
    b) by vendors. You usually purchase programs modified to meet the organization's needs.
    c) in the most economical and practical way to meet deadlines and cost objectives, using internal staff and vendors.

11. Costs for training and WLP are accumulated
    a) on a total aggregate basis only.
    b) on a program-by-program basis.
    c) by specific process components, such as development and delivery, in addition to a specific program.

12. Management involvement in the WLP process is
    a) very low with only occasional input.
    b) moderate, usually by request, or on an as-needed basis.
    c) deliberately planned for all major WLP training activities, to ensure a partnership arrangement.

13. To ensure that WLP is transferred into performance on the job, you
    a) encourage participants to apply what they have learned and report results.
    b) ask managers to support and reinforce training and report results.
    c) use a variety of training transfer strategies appropriate for each situation.

14. The WLP staff's interaction with line management is
    a) rare, you almost never discuss issues with them.
    b) occasional, during activities, such as needs analysis or program coordination.
    c) regular, to build relationships, as well as to develop and deliver programs.

15. WLP's role in major change efforts is
    a) to conduct training to support the project, as required.
    b) to provide administrative support for the program, including training.
    c) to initiate the program, coordinate the overall effort, and measure its progress—in addition to providing training.

16. Most managers view the WLP function as
    a) a questionable function that wastes too much time of employees.
    b) a necessary function that probably cannot be eliminated.
    c) an important resource that can be used to improve the organization.

17. WLP programs are
    a) activity oriented. (All supervisors attend the "Workplace Learning and Performance Workshop.")
    b) individual results-based. (The participant will reduce his or her error rate by at least 20%.)
    c) organizational results-based. (The cost of quality will decrease by 25%.)

18. The investment in WLP is measured primarily by
    a) subjective opinions.
    b) observations by management and reactions from participants.
    c) dollar return through improved productivity, cost savings, or better quality.

19. The WLP effort consists of
    a) usually one-shot, seminar-type approaches.
    b) a full array of courses to meet individual needs.
    c) a variety of WLP programs implemented to bring about change in the organization.

Exercise 1-1. WLP programs assessment (continued).

20. New WLP programs and projects, without some formal method of evaluation, are implemented at your organization
    a) regularly.
    b) seldom.
    c) never.

21. The results of WLP programs are communicated
    a) when requested, to those who have a need to know.
    b) occasionally, to members of management only.
    c) routinely, to a variety of selected target audiences.

22. Management involvement in WLP evaluation
    a) is minor, with no specific responsibilities and few requests.
    b) consists of informal responsibilities for evaluation, with some requests for formal training.
    c) is very specific. All managers have some responsibilities in evaluation.

23. During a business decline at your organization, the WLP function will
    a) be the first to have its staff reduced.
    b) be retained at the same staffing level.
    c) go untouched in staff reductions and possibly beefed up.

24. Budgeting for WLP is based on
    a) last year's budget.
    b) whatever the training department can "sell."
    c) a zero-based system.

25. The principal group that must justify WLP expenditures is
    a) the WLP department.
    b) the human resources or administrative function.
    c) line management.

26. Over the last two years, the WLP budget as a percentage of operating expenses has
    a) decreased.
    b) remained stable.
    c) increased.

27. Top management's involvement in the implementation of WLP programs
    a) is limited to sending invitations, extending congratulations, and passing out certificates.
    b) includes monitoring progress, opening/closing speeches, and presentations on the outlook of the organization.
    c) includes participating in the program to see what's covered, conducting major segments of the program, and requiring key executives to be involved.

28. Line management involvement in conducting WLP programs is
    a) very minor. Only WLP specialists conduct programs.
    b) limited to a few supervisors conducting programs in their area of expertise.
    c) significant. On the average, over half of the programs are conducted by key line managers.

29. When an employee completes a WLP program and returns to the job, his or her supervisor is likely to
    a) make no reference to the program.
    b) ask questions about the program and encourage the use of the material.
    c) require use of the program material and give positive rewards when the material is used successfully.

30. When an employee attends an outside seminar, upon return, he or she is required to
    a) do nothing.
    b) submit a report summarizing the program.
    c) evaluate the seminar, outline plans for implementing the material covered, and estimate the value of the program.

Interpreting the WLP Programs Assessment

Score the assessment instrument as follows:
   1 point for each (a) response
   3 points for each (b) response
   5 points for each (c) response

Score Range	Analysis of Score
120-150	Outstanding environment for achieving results with WLP. Great management support. A truly successful example of results-based WLP.
90-119	Above average in achieving results with WLP. Good management support. A solid and methodical approach to results-based WLP.
60-89	Needs improvement to achieving desired results with WLP. Management support is ineffective. WLP programs do not usually focus on results.
30-59	Serious problems with the success and status of WLP. Management support is non-existent. WLP programs are not producing results.

In the next chapter, you will learn how to create a detailed plan for your evaluation.

2

Plan Your Work

What's Inside This Chapter

This chapter presents the basics in planning your evaluation:

▶ Establishing purpose and feasibility
▶ Defining program objectives
▶ Developing planning documents.

Establishing Purpose and Feasibility

Measuring success and monitoring performance on a routine basis are critical if your stakeholders (as well as you) want to manage programs for results. However, routine evaluation does not mean ROI for all programs all the time. Therefore, the first step in planning your evaluation is to identify its purpose and the feasibility of conducting a comprehensive evaluation including ROI.

Purpose

A clear evaluation purpose helps keep you and your team on track, preventing the project from becoming too overwhelming. Purpose keeps you focused on the "why," providing a basis for using the data once it is generated. All too often, evaluation is done without understanding the purpose of the process; therefore, you let the raw data sit for days, months, and sometimes years before you consider analyzing it to see what happened.

Defining the purpose of the evaluation helps determine the scope of the evaluation project. It drives the type of data to be collected as well as the type of data collection instruments to be used.

Evaluation purposes range from demonstrating value of a particular program to boosting credibility for the entire WLP function. Typical evaluation purposes can be categorized into three overriding themes:

> ▶ Make decisions about programs
> ▶ Improve programs and processes
> ▶ Demonstrate program value.

Make Decisions About Programs. Decisions are made every day, with and without evaluation data. But, with evaluation data, the WLP function can better influence those decisions. Evaluation data can help you make decisions about a program prior to the launch of the program, for example, when you forecast the ROI in a pilot program. Once you know the results of the evaluation, you can decide whether to pursue the program further.

Noted

Decisions are made with or without evaluation data. By providing data, the WLP staff can influence the decision-making process.

Evaluation data can help the WLP staff make decisions about internal development issues. For example, Level 1 data provides information that helps determine the extent to which facilitators need additional skill building. Level 2 data can help you decide whether an additional exercise will better emphasize a skill left undeveloped. Level 3 data not only tells supervisors the extent to which their employees are applying new skills, but also the extent to which events under their control are preventing employees from applying the skills. Levels 4 and 5 data helps senior managers and executives decide whether they will continue investing in certain programs.

The levels of evaluation provide different types of data that influence different decisions. Table 2-1 presents a list of decisions that evaluation data, including ROI, can influence.

Table 2-1. Decisions made with evaluation data.

Decision	Level of Evaluation
WLP staff want to decide whether they should invest in skill development for facilitators.	Level 1
Course designers are concerned the exercises do not cover all learning objectives and need to decide which skills need additional support.	Level 2
Supervisors are uncertain as to whether they want to send employees to future training programs.	Levels 3–4
The WLP clients are deciding if they want to invest in expanding a pilot leadership program for the entire leadership team.	Level 5
Senior managers are planning next year's budget and are concerned about allocating additional funding to the WLP function.	Levels 1–5 (scorecard)
The WLP staff are deciding whether they should eliminate an expensive program that is getting bad reviews from participants, but a senior executive plays golf with the training supplier.	Level 5
A training supplier is trying to convince the WLP team that their leadership program will effectively solve the turnover problem.	Level 5 (forecast/pilot)
Supervisors want to implement a new initiative that will change employee behavior because they believe the WLP program didn't do the job.	Level 3 (focus on barriers and enablers)

Improve Programs and Processes. One of the most important purposes in generating comprehensive data using the ROI methodology is to improve WLP programs and processes. As data is generated, the programs being evaluated can be adjusted so that future presentations are more effective. Reviewing evaluation data in the earlier stages allows the WLP function to implement additional tools and processes that can support the transfer of learning.

Evaluation data can help the WLP function improve its accountability processes. By consistently evaluating programs, the WLP function will find ways to develop data more efficiently through technology or through the use of experts within the organization. Evaluation will also cause the WLP staff to view its programs and processes in a different light, asking questions such as, "Will this prove valuable to the organization?" "Can we get the same results for less cost?" "How can we influence the supervisors to better support this training program?"

Demonstrate Program Value. The ultimate purpose of conducting comprehensive evaluation is to show the value of WLP programs, specifically, the economic value. But, when considering individual programs you plan to evaluate, you often have to ask yourself "value to whom?"

Value is not simply defined. Just as learning occurs at the societal, community, team, and individual levels, value is defined from the perspective of the stakeholder:

- ▶ Is a program valuable to those involved?
- ▶ Is a program valuable to the system that supports it?
- ▶ Is a program economically valuable?

Value can be defined from three perspectives. These perspectives are put into context by comparing them to the five-level ROI framework. Table 2-2 presents these perspectives. The consumer perspective represents the extent to which those involved in the program react positively and acquire some level of knowledge and skills as a result of participating. The system perspective represents the supporting elements within the organization that make the program work. The economic perspective represents the extent to which knowledge or skills transferred to the job positively affect key business measures; when appropriate, these measures are converted to monetary value and compared to the cost of the program to calculate an economic metric, ROI.

Consumer Perspective. The consumers of WLP are those who have an immediate connection with the program. Facilitators, designers, developers, and participants represent consumers. Value to this group is represented at Levels 1 and 2. Data provides the WLP staff feedback so they can make immediate changes to the program as well as decide where developmental needs exist. This data provides the participants a look at what the group thought about the program and how they each fared from a knowledge and skills acquisition perspective compared to the group. Some measures—those representing utility of knowledge gain—are often used to predict actual application of knowledge and skills.

Table 2-2. Value perspectives.

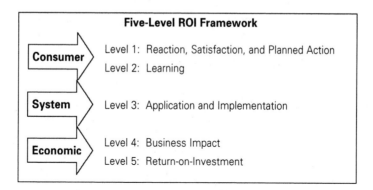

System Perspective. The system represents those people and functions that support learning within an organization. This includes participant supervisors; participant peers and team members; executives; and support functions, such as the IT department or the WLP function. In many cases, the system is represented by the client.

Though Level 3 data provides evidence of participant application of newly acquired knowledge and skills, the greatest value in evaluating at this level is in determining the extent to which the system supports learning transfer. This is determined by the barriers and enablers identified through the Level 3 evaluation.

Economic Perspective. The economic perspective is typically that of the client—the person or group funding the program. Although certainly the supervisor is interested in whether the program influenced business outcomes and the ROI, it is the client—who is sometimes the supervisor, but more often senior management—who makes the financial investment in the program. Levels 4 and 5 provide data representing the economic value of the investment.

Table 2-3 presents the value perspectives compared to the frequency of use of the data provided by each level of evaluation. Although there is value at all levels, the lower levels of evaluation are implemented most frequently. This is due to the feasibility of conducting evaluations at the lower levels versus the higher levels.

Feasibility

Program evaluations have multiple purposes—when you evaluate at Level 5 to influence funding decisions, you still need Level 1 data to help you improve delivery and design. This is one reason the lower levels of evaluation are conducted more often

Table 2-3. Value perspective versus use.

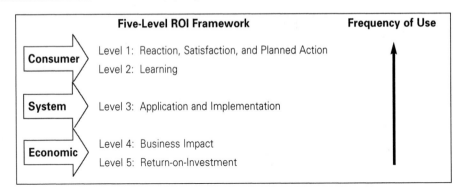

than the higher levels. Other drivers that determine the feasibility of evaluating programs to the various levels include the program objectives, the availability of data, and the appropriateness for ROI.

Program Objectives. Program objectives are the fundamental basis for evaluation. Program objectives drive the design and development of the program and define how to measure success. Program objectives define what the program is intended to do and how to measure participant achievement and system support of the learning transfer process. All too often, however, minimal emphasis is placed on developing objectives and their defined measures.

Availability of Data. Can you get the information you need to determine if the objectives are met? Availability of data at Levels 1 and 2 is rarely a concern. Simply ask the opinion of the program participants, test them, or facilitate role plays and exercises to assess their overall understanding. Level 3 data is often obtained by going to participants, their supervisors, their peers, and their subordinates. The challenge is in the availability of Level 4 data. Are measures being monitored on a routine basis? If not, who or what is the best source of this information and how can you collect it?

Program objectives and data availability are key drivers in determining the feasibility of evaluating a program to ROI; however, some programs are just inappropriate for ROI.

Appropriateness for ROI. How do you know if a program is appropriate for ROI evaluation? By answering yes to the following three questions:

1. Can the effects of the program on a measure be isolated from other influences?
2. Can Level 4 measures be converted to monetary value?
3. Does the profile of the program meet specific criteria?

The first question represents the most important, yet, most misunderstood step in the ROI process—isolating the effects of the program. More often than not, researchers, practitioners, and experts in other areas of WLP will question the feasibility and appropriateness of this step. But, if you report business impact or ROI in programs without taking this step, the information is invalid. If you suggest that your sales program generated enough profit to overcome the costs of the program resulting in a 100% ROI, someone in the organization will ask, "How do you know it was your sales training program that generated that profit?"

There are a variety of ways to isolate the effects of programs. Control group methodology is only one—and often the least feasible. If you do not intend to take this step in the process, then don't report business impact or ROI. You'll be kidding yourself as to the program's effect on the organization, and you'll be setting yourself up for loss of credibility.

The next question is fundamental in moving from Level 4 to Level 5—converting data to monetary value. Omit this step, and you cannot report ROI. As discussed earlier, ROI is an economic indicator comparing monetary benefits of a program to the fully loaded costs. If you cannot convert a measure to monetary value, the benefit is reported as intangible (still an important benefit, just not one that will be included in the ROI calculation).

There are a variety of ways to calculate monetary value for impact measures: standard values, historical costs, expert opinion, estimations, previous studies, and more. The key is converting the measure credibly.

The third question to consider in assessing the appropriateness of a program in going to ROI is the program profile—does it meet specific criteria? An inexpensive program offered one time, never to be offered again, is not suitable for ROI. Why invest resources in conducting such a comprehensive evaluation on a program for which the data serves no valuable or ongoing purpose? Basic skill building is not always suitable for ROI, for example, basic computer skills. Sometimes you just want to know that participants know how to do something rather than what the impact of their doing it has on the organization. Induction programs are not always suitable for ROI, especially entry level programs in which participants are just beginning their professional careers.

So what programs are suitable for ROI? Those programs that are

- expected to have a long life cycle
- linked to organization strategy
- connected to organization objectives
- expensive, requiring resources, time, and money
- targeted to a large audience
- highly visible throughout the organization
- of interest to management
- intended to drive major change within the organization.

In a recent study of best practice organizations using the ROI methodology, it was uncovered that those organizations who successfully implement the process evaluate 5% to 10% of their programs to Level 5, ROI. Considering the number of programs offered in any given organization, this is a feasible target. Table 2-4 presents targets suggested by the authors of this book, established by the Government Accountability Office (GAO), identified through a research study on the development and implementation of training evaluation in the public sector (federal, state, and local government), and established by Wachovia Bank. These targets can serve as a guide as you develop your strategy for implementing ROI.

Table 2-4. Percentage of programs evaluated at each level.

Level	Targets	GAO	Public Sector Survey	Wachovia
1	100%	100%	72%	100%
2	60%	60%	32%	50%
3	30%	30%	20%	30%
4	10%–20%	10%	12%	10%
5	5%–10%	5%	5%	5%

Noted

Not all programs are suitable for ROI; but when you want to go to ROI, you must isolate the effects of the program from other influences and credibly convert data to monetary value.

Defining Program Objectives

Before the evaluation begins, the program objectives must be developed. Program objectives are linked to the needs assessment. When a problem is identified, the needs assessment process begins. Assessments are conducted to determine exactly what the problem is; how on-the-job performance change can resolve the problem; what knowledge or skills need to be acquired to change on-the-job performance; and how best to present the solution so that those involved, the consumers, can acquire the knowledge and skills to change performance to solve the business problem. From here, program objectives are developed to help guide program designers and developers, provide guidance to facilitators, provide goals for participants, and provide a framework for evaluators.

Program objectives reflect the same five-level framework used in categorizing evaluation data. The key in writing program objectives is to be specific in identifying measures of success. All too often, very broad program objectives are written. While this is acceptable in the initial phases of program design, it is the specific measures of success that drive results and serve as the basis for the evaluation.

Level 1 Reaction, Satisfaction, and Planned Action Objectives

Level 1 objectives are critical in that they describe expected immediate and long-term satisfaction with a program. They describe issues that are important to the success of the program, including facilitation, relevance and importance of content, logistics, and intended use of knowledge and skills. But, there has been criticism of the Level 1 evaluation. This criticism surrounds the use of the Level 1 overall satisfaction as a measure of success. The overuse of the overall satisfaction measure has led many organizations to make funding decisions based on whether participants like a program, later realizing the data was misleading.

Level 1 objectives should identify issues that are important and measurable rather than esoteric indicators that provide limited useful information. They should be attitude based, clearly worded, and specific. Level 1 objectives specify that the participant has changed in thinking or perception as a result of the program and underscore the linkage between attitude and the success of the program. While Level 1 objectives represent a satisfaction index from the consumer perspective, these objectives should also have the capability to predict program success. Given these criteria, it is important that Level 1 objectives are represented by specific measures of success.

A good predictor of the application of knowledge and skills is the perceived relevance by participants of program content. So, a Level 1 objective may be

At the end of the course, participants will perceive program content as relevant to their jobs.

A question remains, however: "How will you know you are successful with this objective?" This is where a good measure comes in. Table 2-5 compares the broad objective with the more specific measure.

Table 2-5. Compare broad objective with more specific measure.

Objective	Measure
At the end of the course, participants will perceive program content as relevant to their jobs.	80% of participants rate *program relevance* a 4.5 out of 5 on a Likert scale.

Now, for those of you who are more research driven, you might want to take this a step further by defining (literally) what you mean by "relevance." Relevance may be defined as:

▶ knowledge and skills that participants can immediately apply in their work
▶ knowledge and skills reflective of participants' day-to-day work activity.

If this is the case, the measures of success are even more detailed. Table 2-6 compares the broad objective to the more detailed measures. Success with these two measures can be reported individually, or you can combine the results of the two measures to create a "relevance index."

Breaking down objectives to specific measures provides a clearer picture of success; however, it also lengthens your Level 1 data collection instrument and requires more

Table 2-6. Compare broad objective with more detailed measures.

Objective	Measures
At the end of the course, participants will perceive program content as relevant to their jobs.	80% of participants indicate that they can *immediately apply the knowledge and skills in their work* as indicated by rating this measure a 4.5 out of 5 on a Likert scale.
	80% of participants view the knowledge and skills as *reflective of their day-to-day work activity* as indicated by rating this measure 4.5 out of 5 on a Likert scale.

Think About This

Overall satisfaction is often referred to as a measure of how much participants liked the cookies offered during a WLP program. Recent analysis of a comprehensive Level 1 end-of-course questionnaire showed the participants viewed the program as less than relevant, not useful, and they had little intention to use what they learned. Scores included

- Knowledge and skills presented are relevant to my job.   2.8 out of 5
- Knowledge and skills presented will be useful to my work.   2.6 out of 5
- I intend to use what I learned in this course.   2.2 out of 5

Surprisingly, however, respondents scored the overall satisfaction measure as, "I am satisfied with the program," 4.6 out of 5. Hmmmm, it must have been the cookies!

analysis. The question to consider is, "Do you really need this detail in your measures?" For a program planned for ROI evaluation, no. Simple, but specific Level 1 objectives and measures of success are sufficient when evaluating a program to ROI. Conserve your resources for the more challenging tasks of Level 4 and Level 5 evaluation.

Basic Rule 2

When an evaluation is planned for a higher level, the previous level of evaluation does not have to be comprehensive.

Level 2 Learning Objectives

There is increased interest in evaluating the acquisition of knowledge and skills. These drivers include growth in the number of learning organizations, emphasis being placed on intellectual capital, and increased use of certifications as a discriminator in the selection process. Given this, Level 2 objectives should be well defined.

Level 2 objectives communicate expected outcomes from instruction; they describe competent performance that should be the result of learning. The best learning objectives describe behaviors that are observable and measurable. As with Level 1 objectives, Level 2 objectives are outcome based. Clearly worded and specific, they spell out what the participant must be able to do as a result of learning.

There are three types of learning objectives:

1. Awareness—participants are familiar with terms, concepts, and processes.
2. Knowledge—participants have a general understanding of concepts and processes.
3. Performance—participants are able to demonstrate the knowledge and skills acquired.

A typical learning objective may be

At the end of the program participants will be able to implement Microsoft Word.

Sounds reasonable. But, what does successful implementation look like? How will you know you have achieved success? You need a measure, as shown in table 2-7. Now, you can evaluate the success of learning.

Table 2-7. Compare broad objective with implementation measures.

Objective	Measures
At the end of the course, participants will be able to implement Microsoft Word.	Within a 10-minute time period, participants will be able to demonstrate to the facilitator the following applications of Microsoft Word with zero errors: • File, Save as, Save as Web Page • Format, including font, paragraph, background, and themes • Insert tables, add columns and rows, and delete columns and rows.

Level 3 Application and Implementation Objectives

Where learning objectives and their specific measures of success tell you what participants can do, Level 3 objectives tell you what participants are expected to do when they leave the learning environment. Application objectives describe the expected outputs of the WLP program. They describe competent performance that should be the result of training and provide the basis for evaluating on-the-job performance changes. The emphasis is placed on applying what was learned.

The best Level 3 objectives identify behaviors that are observable and measurable, outcome based, clearly worded, specific, and spell out what the participant has changed as a result of the learning.

A typical application objective might read something like this:

Participants will use effective meeting behaviors.

Again, you need specifics in order to evaluate success. What are effective meeting behaviors and to what degree should participants use those skills? Some examples of measures are shown in table 2-8. With defined measures, you now know what success looks like.

Table 2-8. Compare application objective with measurable behaviors.

Objective	Measures
Participants will use effective meeting behaviors.	Participants will develop a detailed agenda outlining the specific topics to be covered for 100% of meetings.
	Participants will establish meeting ground rules at the beginning of 100% of meetings.
	Participants will follow up on meeting action items within three days following 100% of meetings.

An important element of Level 3 evaluation is that this is where you can assess success with learning transfer. Is the system supporting learning? Here you look for barriers to application as well as supporting elements (enablers). It is critical to gather data around these issues so that corrective action can be taken when evidence of a problem exists. You may ask how you can influence issues outside your control—say, when participants indicate that it is the supervisor that prevents them from applying newly acquired knowledge.

Through the evaluation process, data is developed that arms you to engage in dialogue with supervisors. Bring the supervisor into the fold; ask the supervisor for help. Tell the supervisors that there is evidence that some supervisors do not support learning opportunities and you need their advice as how to remedy the situation.

A comprehensive assessment at Level 3 provides you with tools to begin the dialogue with all stakeholders. Through this dialogue you may find that many managers and supervisors and colleagues in other departments do not understand the role of WLP, nor do they have a clear understanding of the adult learning process. This is an opportunity to teach them, thereby, increasing their support.

Level 4 Business Impact Objectives

Success with Level 4 objectives is critical when you want to achieve a positive ROI for the WLP investment. Level 4 objectives provide the basis for measuring the consequences of application of skills and knowledge and place emphasis on achieving bottom-line results. The best impact measures contain measures that are both linked to the skills and knowledge in the program and easily collected. Level 4 objectives are results based, clearly worded, and specific. They spell out what the participant has accomplished in the business unit as a result of the program. Four types of impact objectives involving hard data are

▶ output focused
▶ quality focused
▶ cost focused
▶ time focused.

Three common types of impact measures involving soft data are

▶ customer service focused
▶ work climate focused
▶ work habits focused.

Following is an example. As reported in the article "Brewers Get into the Spirits of Marketing," (*USA Today*, Howard, T., p. 1B, May 16, 2005), the beer industry is losing market share to the high-end spirits. A large U.S. brewery implements a marketing strategy including new ads showing a sleek, silver "Love Train" delivering beer to upscale partiers. Table 2-9 shows the objective and a potential measure.

Here is another example: A large, multinational computer manufacturer prides itself on the quality of the computer systems purchased and the service provided

Table 2-9. Compare impact objective with measure.

Objective	Measure
Increase market share.	Increase market share of young professionals by 10% within nine months of new ad launch.

when there is a problem. The company makes it easy for purchasers to get assistance by selling lucrative warranties on all of its products. One particular system, the X-1350, comes with a three-year warranty that includes the "gold standard" for technical support for an additional $105.

In the past year, there has been an increase in the number of call-outs to repair contractors, particularly with regard to the X-1350. This increase is costing the company not only money, but also customer satisfaction. A new program is implemented to improve the quality of the computer. Table 2-10 shows the objective and specific measures of success.

Table 2-10. Compare impact objective for quality improvement with measures.

Objective	Measures
Improve the quality of the X-1350.	Reduce the number of warranty claims on the X-1350 by 10% within six months after the program.
	Improve overall customer satisfaction with quality of the X-1350 by 10% as indicated by customer satisfaction survey taken six months after the program.
	Achieve top scores on product quality measures included in industry quality survey.

Detailed measures describe the meaning of success. They also serve as the basis for the questions that you ask during the evaluation.

Level 5 ROI Objectives

The Level 5 objectives target the specific economic return anticipated when an investment is made in a program. This objective defines "good" when asked, "What is a good ROI?" There are four options when considering the target ROI:

1. Set the ROI at the level of other investments.
2. Set the ROI at a higher standard.

3. Set the ROI at break-even.

4. Set the ROI based on client expectations.

Set ROI at the Level of Other Investments. Setting ROI at the same level of other investments is not uncommon. Many WLP groups use this approach to ensure a linkage with operations. To establish this target, check with finance and accounting, and ask what the average return is for other investments.

Set ROI at a Higher Standard. Another approach to establishing the Level 5 objectives is to raise the bar for WLP. Set the target ROI at a higher level than the other investments. Because WLP affects so many and contributes so much to the organization, a higher than normal expected ROI is not unreasonable.

Set ROI at Break-Even. Some organizations are satisfied with a 0% ROI—break-even. This says that the organization got the investment back. For instance, if an organization spends $50,000 on a particular program, the monetary benefit was the $50,000. There was no gain, but the investment came back. Many organizations, such as nonprofit, community, and faith-based, value the break-even ROI.

Set ROI Based on Client Expectations. A final strategy to setting the Level 5 objective is to ask the client. Remember that the client is the person or group that is funding the program. The client may be willing to invest in a program given a certain return on that investment.

Developing the Plans

There are two basic documents that you will complete when planning your ROI impact study. These are the data collection plan and the ROI analysis plan. By completing these plans thoroughly, you will be well on your way to conducting an ROI study. Once completed, have the client sign off on your approach to the evaluation. By taking this important step, you gain buy-in and the confidence of knowing that you have support for your planned approach.

Data Collection Plan

The data collection plan lays the initial groundwork for the ROI study. This plan holds the answers to the questions:

- ▶ What do you ask?
- ▶ How do you ask?

- Whom do you ask?
- When do you ask?
- Who does the asking?

What Do You Ask? The answers to this question lie in the program objectives and their respective measures. Specific measurable objectives and measures of success serve as the basis for the questions you intend to ask. When broad objectives are developed, the measures must be clearly described so that you know when success is achieved.

How Do You Ask? How you ask is dependent on a variety of issues, including resources available to collect data. Level 1 data is typically approached using the end-of-course questionnaire. To collect Level 2 data, use tests, role plays, self-assessments, and facilitator assessments. Follow-up data collection (Levels 3 and 4) is the most challenging; however, there are a variety of options, including questionnaires, focus groups, interviews, action plans, and performance monitoring. These options provide flexibility and ensure that the lack of data collection methods is not a barrier to following up on program application and impact.

Whom Do You Ask? Your source of data is critical. You will go only to the most credible source; sometimes this includes multiple sources. The more sources providing data, the more reliable the data. The only condition is the cost of going to those multiple sources.

When Do You Ask? Timing of data collection is critical and getting it right is sometimes a challenge. You want to wait long enough for new behaviors to have had time to become routine, but not so long that the participants forget how they developed the new behavior. You also want to wait long enough for impact to occur, but most executives aren't willing to wait an extended period of time. Therefore, you have to pick a point in time at which you believe application and impact have occurred.

Who Does the Asking? Who will be responsible for each step in the data collection process? Typically, the facilitator collects data at Levels 1 and 2. For the higher levels of evaluation, representatives of the evaluation team are assigned specific roles. One of these roles is data collection. A person or team is assigned to the task of developing the data collection instrument and administering it. This includes developing a strategy to ensure a successful response rate. Table 2-11 presents an example of the completed data collection plan.

Table 2-11. Completed data collection plan.

Program: _____ Effective Meetings   Responsibility: _____   Date: _____

Level	Program Objectives	Measures of Success	Data Collection Method	Data Sources	Timing	Responsibilities
1	**REACTION/SATISFACTION AND PLANNED ACTIONS** • Positive reaction • Planned actions	• Average rating of at least 4.0 on 5.0 scale on quality, usefulness, and achievement of program objectives • 100% submit planned actions	• End-of-course questionnaire • Completed action plans	• Participants	• End of course	• Facilitator
2	**LEARNING** • Identify the extent and cost of meetings • Identify positives, negatives, and implications of basic meeting issues and dynamics • Acquisition of effective meeting behaviors	• Given cost guidelines, identify the cost of the last three meetings • From a list of 30 positive and negative meeting behaviors, correctly identify the implications of each behavior • Demonstrate appropriate response to eight of 10 active role-play scenarios	• Meeting profile • Written test • Skill practice observation	• Participants	• At the beginning of the program (pre) • At the end of the program (post) • During program	• Facilitator

3	**APPLICATION/ IMPLEMENTATION** • Use of effective meeting behaviors • Barriers • Enablers	• Reported change in behavior to planning and conducting meetings • Number and variety of barriers • Number and variety of enablers	• Action plan • Questionnaire (for three groups)	• Participants	• Three months	• Program owner
4	**BUSINESS IMPACT** • Time savings from fewer meetings, shorter meetings, and fewer participants (hours savings per month) • Variety of business results measures from more successful meetings	• Time savings • Time savings, cost savings, output improvement, quality improvement, project turnaround, as reported	• Questionnaire (for three groups)	• Participants	• Three months	• Program owner
5	**ROI** Target ROI at least 25%	Comments: _____				

Source: Phillips, J.J., and P.P. Phillips. (2005). *ROI at Work*. Alexandria, VA: ASTD Press.

ROI Analysis Plan

The second planning document is the ROI analysis plan, which requires that you identify

- ▶ methods for isolating the effects of the program
- ▶ methods for converting data to monetary value
- ▶ cost categories
- ▶ intangible benefits
- ▶ communication targets for the final report
- ▶ other influences and issues during application
- ▶ comments.

The ROI analysis plan also includes a column for comments or any notes that you might need to take regarding the evaluation process.

Methods for Isolating the Effects of the Program. Decide the technique you plan to use to isolate the effects of the program on your Level 4 measures. Typically, the method of isolation is the same for all measures, but often you find in working with some measures that you can use one technique, whereas working with other measures you may have to use another technique.

Methods for Converting Data to Monetary Value. Next, complete the column identifying the methods to convert your Level 4 measures to monetary value. In some cases, you will choose not to convert a measure to monetary value. When that is the case, just leave that space blank. Otherwise, select a technique described in chapter 5.

Cost Categories. This section includes all costs for the program. These costs include the needs assessment, program design and development, program delivery, evaluation costs, and some amount representative of overhead and administrative costs for those people and processes that support your programs. Each cost category is listed on the ROI analysis plan.

Intangible Benefits. Not all measures will be converted to monetary value. There is a four-part test that helps you decide which measures to convert and which not to convert. Those measures you choose not to convert to monetary value are considered intangible benefits. Move the Level 4 measures that you don't convert to monetary value to this column.

Communication Targets for the Final Report. In many cases, organizations will plan their communication targets in detail. Here, during the evaluation-planning phase, you will identify at a minimum those audiences to whom the final report will be submitted. Four key audiences always get a copy or summary of the report: the participants, WLP staff, supervisors of the participants, and client.

Other Influences and Issues During Application. This column provides an opportunity to anticipate any issues that may occur during the training process that might have a negative effect or no effect on your identified impact measures. You can also use this column to list issues that might occur that could negatively affect the evaluation process.

Comments. The final column on the ROI analysis plan is for comments. Here, you can put notes to remind yourself and your evaluation team of key issues, comments regarding potential success or failure of the program, reminders for specific tasks to be conducted by the evaluation team, and so forth.

The importance of planning your data collection for your ROI analysis cannot be stressed enough. By planning in detail what you are going to ask, how you are going to ask, who you are going to ask, when you are going to ask, and who will do the asking, along with the key steps in the ROI analysis, will help ensure successful execution. Additionally, having clients sign off on your plans will ensure support when the evaluation results are presented. Table 2-12 is a completed ROI analysis plan.

Getting It Done

Now it is time for you to go to work. Before you go any further in this book, select a program that is suitable for ROI.

If this is your first ROI study, consider selecting a program in which you are confident that success will be achieved. Success with your first study is an incentive for the next one.

Once you have identified the program, answer the following questions. From here, you will begin developing the data collection plan.

Program: _____

Evaluation Team: _____

Expected Date of Completion: _____

1. What is your purpose in conducting an ROI evaluation on this program?

2. What are the program objectives at each level of evaluation?

Level 1 _____

Level 2 _____

Level 3 _____

Level 4 _____

Level 5 _____

3. What are your measures of success for each objective?

Level 1 _____

Level 2 _____

Level 3 _____

Level 4 _____

Level 5 _____

4. Transfer your answers to questions 2 and 3 to the first two columns in the data collection
   plan in table 2-13.

In the next chapter, you will learn methods for collecting data and will complete the data collection plan.

Table 2-12. Completed ROI analysis plan.

Program: _____   Responsibility: _____   Date: _____

Effective Meetings

Data Items (Usually Level 4)	Methods for Isolating the Effects of the Program/Process	Methods of Converting Data to Monetary Values	Cost Categories	Intangible Benefits	Communication Targets for Final Report	Other Influences/Issues During Application	Comments
• Time savings	• Participants' estimates	• Hourly wage and benefits	• Program fee per participant	• Improvement in individual productivity not captured elsewhere	• Business unit president	• Participants must see need for providing measurement	Participants will identify specific improvements as a result of meetings being conducted more effectively
• Miscellaneous business measures	• Participants' estimates	• Participants' estimates (using standard values when available)	• Travel/lodging/meals	• Stress reduction	• Senior managers	• Follow-up process will be explained to participants during program	
			• Facilities	• Improved planning and scheduling	• Managers of participants	• Three groups will be measured	
			• Participants' salaries plus benefits	• Greater participation in meetings	• Participants		
					• Training and development staff		

Source: Phillips, J.J., and P.P. Phillips. (2005). *ROI at Work*. Alexandria, VA: ASTD Press.

Table 2-13. Blank data collection plan.

Program: _____ Evaluation Project Lead: _____ Date: _____

Level	Program Objectives	Measures of Success	Data Collection Method	Data Sources	Timing	Responsibilities
1	REACTION/SATISFACTION AND PLANNED ACTIONS					
2	LEARNING					
3	APPLICATION/ IMPLEMENTATION					
4	BUSINESS IMPACT					
5	ROI					

Comments: _____

Source: The ROI Institute.

3

Collect Data

■ ■

What's Inside This Chapter

This chapter presents the basics in collecting data for your ROI study, which includes:

▶ Selecting the data collection method
▶ Defining the source of data
▶ Determining the time of data collection.

Selecting the Method

A variety of data collection techniques exist to assist in collecting the right data from the right source at the right time. The most often used data collection technique is the end-of-course questionnaire used to collect Level 1 data. The end-of-course questionnaire collects data that answers questions related to:

▶ course relevance to the job
▶ course importance to the job
▶ participant intent to use knowledge and skills learned
▶ amount of new information offered through the course
▶ participant willingness to recommend the course to others.

End-of-course questionnaires can also prod participants to think about potential uses of what they have learned in the WLP program as well as the effect these potential uses will have on the organization. Table 3-1 presents a sample end-of-course questionnaire.

Table 3-1. End-of-course questionnaire.

Leading Change in Organizations

Thank you for participating in Leading Change in Organizations. As promised, you have the opportunity to provide feedback as to how we can improve this course.

Please respond to the following questions regarding your perception of the program as well as your anticipated use of the skills learned during the program. We also would like to know how you think the skills applied from this course will affect business measures important to your function.

You will receive a summary of these results by June 6.

I. Your reaction to course facilitation	Strongly Disagree			Strongly Agree	
	1	2	3	4	5
1. The instructor was knowledgeable about the subject.	☐	☐	☐	☐	☐
2. The instructor was prepared for the class.	☐	☐	☐	☐	☐
3. Participants were encouraged to take part in class discussions.	☐	☐	☐	☐	☐
4. The instructor was responsive to participants' questions.	☐	☐	☐	☐	☐
5. The instructor's energy and enthusiasm kept the participants actively engaged.	☐	☐	☐	☐	☐
6. The instructor discussed how I can apply the skills and knowledge taught in the class.	☐	☐	☐	☐	☐
II. Your reaction to the course content					
7. The course content is relevant to my current job.	☐	☐	☐	☐	☐
8. The course content is important to my current job.	☐	☐	☐	☐	☐
9. The material was organized logically.	☐	☐	☐	☐	☐
10. The exercises and examples helped me understand the material.	☐	☐	☐	☐	☐
11. The course content provided me new information.	☐	☐	☐	☐	☐
12. I intend to use what I learned in this course.	☐	☐	☐	☐	☐
III. New knowledge and skills acquired in the course					
13. I learned new knowledge and skills from this course.	☐	☐	☐	☐	☐
14. I am confident that I can effectively apply the skills learned in the course.	☐	☐	☐	☐	☐

IV. Your expected application of knowledge and skills

	Strongly Disagree				Strongly Agree
	1	2	3	4	5
15. I will effectively apply what I have learned in this course.	☐	☐	☐	☐	☐

16. What percentage of your total work time requires the knowledge and skills presented in this course?

☐ 0% ☐ 10% ☐ 20% ☐ 30% ☐ 40% ☐ 50% ☐ 60% ☐ 70% ☐ 80% ☐ 90% ☐ 100%

17. On a scale of 0% (not at all) to 100% (extremely critical), how critical is applying the content of this course to your job success?

☐ 0% ☐ 10% ☐ 20% ☐ 30% ☐ 40% ☐ 50% ☐ 60% ☐ 70% ☐ 80% ☐ 90% ☐ 100%

18. What percentage of the new knowledge and skills learned from this course do you estimate you will directly apply to your job?

☐ 0% ☐ 10% ☐ 20% ☐ 30% ☐ 40% ☐ 50% ☐ 60% ☐ 70% ☐ 80% ☐ 90% ☐ 100%

19. What potential barriers could prevent you from applying the knowledge and skills learned from this course? _____

_____

20. What potential enablers will support you in applying the knowledge and skills learned from this course?

_____

_____

V. How what you learned will impact the business

21. As a result of your applying the knowledge and skills learned in this course, to what extent will the following measures be improved?

	Not at all				Completely
	1	2	3	4	5
Productivity	☐	☐	☐	☐	☐
Sales	☐	☐	☐	☐	☐
Quality	☐	☐	☐	☐	☐
Costs	☐	☐	☐	☐	☐
Time	☐	☐	☐	☐	☐
Job Satisfaction	☐	☐	☐	☐	☐
Customer Satisfaction	☐	☐	☐	☐	☐

Because Level 1 data also includes planned actions, an action plan can be used to gather information about specific actions intended to be taken by participants; however, this action plan is not to be confused with that used in collecting follow-up data. Rather the Level 1 action plan requires participants to list the planned actions and completion dates; there is no intended follow-up. Table 3-2 presents an example. Note that these questions can also be built into the end-of-course questionnaire.

Table 3-2. Action plan.

Action Plan
Name:_____ Date: _____
Course: _____ Instructor:_____

	Planned Actions	Completion Date
1.	_____	_____
2.	_____	_____
3.	_____	_____
4.	_____	_____
5.	_____	_____

At Level 2, data is collected using a variety of techniques to determine if learning occurred. Fundamental questions answered at Level 2 represent

- ▶ new knowledge and skills acquired
- ▶ improvement in knowledge and skills
- ▶ confidence to apply knowledge and skills.

While it is sometimes assumed testing is the only technique to measure skill and knowledge acquisition, there are many other techniques to gather this information. These include

- ▶ written tests and exercises
- ▶ criterion reference tests
- ▶ performance demonstrations
- ▶ performance observations
- ▶ case studies
- ▶ simulations
- ▶ peer assessments
- ▶ self assessments
- ▶ skill- and confidence-building exercises.

The data collection challenge with regard to applying the ROI methodology comes with the follow-up—gathering data represented in the higher levels of evaluation.

Postprogram Data Collection Methods

Postprogram data represents those measures of success categorized as Levels 3, 4, and 5. Level 3 follow-up data represents the extent to which participants apply the knowledge and skills learned in the course. Fundamentally, this level of data addresses issues related to participants':

- effectiveness in applying knowledge and skills
- frequency in applying knowledge and skills
- barriers to applying knowledge and skills
- enablers supporting application of knowledge and skills.

Data collected at Level 4 represents follow-up data that addresses the consequence of participants' application of the knowledge and skills. This data serves to report the results of the program on measures of:

- output
- quality
- cost
- time
- job satisfaction
- customer satisfaction
- work habits and attitudes.

At Level 5, the new data collected is the cost data. Cost data is derived from organization records, supplier records, WLP staff, and participants. Table 3-3 summarizes follow-up data collection techniques.

The most often used methods of data collection for ROI evaluation are questionnaires, interviews, focus groups, action plans, and performance records.

Questionnaires. Questionnaires are the most often used data collection technique when conducting an ROI evaluation. Questionnaires are inexpensive and easy to administer. Depending on the length, they take very little of respondents' time. Questionnaires can be sent via mail, internal mail, email, or can be distributed online either posted on an intranet or via one of any number of electronic survey tools available on the Internet.

Table 3-3. Data collection techniques.

	Level 3	Level 4	Level 5
Follow-Up Survey	✓		
Follow-Up Questionnaire	✓	✓	
Follow-Up Interviews	✓		
Follow-Up Focus Groups	✓		
Program Assignments	✓		
Action Planning	✓	✓	
Performance Contracting	✓	✓	
Program Follow-Up Session	✓	✓	
Performance Monitoring	✓	✓	
Cost Data			✓

Questionnaires also provide versatility in the types of data that you can collect. You can collect data about the demographics of participants, attitudes toward the program, knowledge gained during the program, and how the participants have applied that knowledge. In the questionnaire, you can ask respondents to tell how much a particular measure is worth. Participants, through a questionnaire, can tell how much a measure has improved. They can identify other variables that influenced improvements in a given measure, and they can tell the extent of the influence of those variables.

Questions in a questionnaire can be open-ended, closed, or forced-choice. Participants may be asked to select multiple responses or one response from an array of options. Likert scale questions are very common in follow-up questionnaires as are frequency scales, ordinal scales, and paired-comparison scales, along with comparative scales and linear numeric scales. Periodically, you'll see an adjective checklist on a questionnaire—just to give the participants the opportunity to reinforce their attitude toward the program.

While questionnaires can be quite lengthy and you can ask any number of questions, the best questionnaires are those that are concise. They reflect those questions that will allow you to gather needed data. Do not sacrifice thoroughness for brevity, however; ensure that you cover all the issues necessary to develop needed information. Table 3-4 provides a simple questionnaire, focused on gathering Level 4 data after the implementation of a coaching intervention. This simple and brief questionnaire is quite powerful when used to understand the impact of a program and to have participants provide information on both isolating the effects of the intervention and converting data to monetary values.

Table 3-4. Sample data collection instrument, Level 4.

Coaching Questions

1. To what extent did coaching positively influence the following measures:

	Significant Influence				No Influence	
	5	4	3	2	1	n/a
Productivity	☐	☐	☐	☐	☐	☐
Sales	☐	☐	☐	☐	☐	☐
Quality	☐	☐	☐	☐	☐	☐
Cost	☐	☐	☐	☐	☐	☐
Efficiency	☐	☐	☐	☐	☐	☐
Time	☐	☐	☐	☐	☐	☐
Employee Satisfaction	☐	☐	☐	☐	☐	☐
Customer Satisfaction	☐	☐	☐	☐	☐	☐

2. What other measures were positively influenced by coaching?

   _____

3. Of the measures listed above, improvement in which one is most directly linked to coaching? (Check only one)

   ☐ productivity   ☐ sales   ☐ quality
   ☐ cost   ☐ efficiency   ☐ time
   ☐ employee satisfaction   ☐ customer satisfaction

4. Please define the measure above and its unit for measurement.

   _____

5. How much did the measure identified in questions 3 and 4 improve since you began this process?

   ☐ weekly   ☐ monthly   ☐ annually

6. What other processes, programs, or events may have contributed to this improvement?

   _____

7. Recognizing that other factors may have caused this improvement, estimate the percentage of improvement related directly to coaching?

   _____%

8. For this measure, what is the monetary value of improvement for one unit of this measure? Although this is difficult, please make every effort to estimate the value.

   _____

(continued on page 54)

Table 3-4. Sample data collection instrument, Level 4 (continued).

9. Please state your basis for the estimated value of improvement you indicated above.

_____

_____

_____

10. What is the annual value of improvement in the measure you selected above?

_____

_____

11. What confidence do you place in the estimates you have provided in the prior questions? 0% is no confidence, 100% is certainty.

_____%

Interviews. Interviews are probably the most ideal method of data collection. Interviews allow you to get more precise and accurate data than questionnaires, action plans, and even focus groups. Interviews can be conducted in person or over the telephone. Those interviews conducted in person have the greatest advantage because the person conducting the interview can show the respondent items that can help clarify questions and response options. It also allows the person conducting the interview to observe any body language that may indicate that the respondent is uncomfortable with the question, anxious because of time commitments, or not interested in the interview process. Unlike the situation with a paper-based or email questionnaire where the disinterested respondent can simply throw away the questionnaire or press the delete key, in an interview setting, the evaluator can change strategies, in hopes of motivating respondents to participate. Interviews are used when the evaluator needs to ask complex questions or the list of response choices is so long that it becomes confusing if administered through a questionnaire. In-person interviews are conducted when the information collected through the interview process is considered confidential or when the respondent would feel uncomfortable providing the information on paper or over the telephone.

Interviews can be structured or unstructured. Unstructured interviews allow greater depth of dialog between the evaluator and the respondent. Structured interviews work exactly like a questionnaire, except that there is a face-to-face rapport between the evaluator and the respondent. The respondent has the opportunity to elaborate on responses, and the evaluator can ask follow-up questions for clarification.

Telephone interviews are strictly for convenience, although some respondents prefer to talk over the telephone. Interview questions can be emailed prior to the telephone call. The disadvantage of telephone interviews is that the personal rapport is not as great as in face-to-face interviews, and the respondent does not have the advantage of the evaluator showing or referring to specific items to clarify issues.

Although interviews provide the most accurate data, they are the most costly and you need to consider how many interviews are needed to gather the appropriate amount of data. In many cases, interviews are conducted only with executives or supervisors of the participant, providing supplementary data. This minimizes the number of people with whom you need to speak. As you know, scheduling interviews can be a challenge and getting through the executive's gatekeeper can prove even a greater challenge than putting the interview on the executive's schedule once you do make it through. If possible, depending on the cost of the program and how much you want to spend on the evaluation, you might consider hiring a professional interviewer. At the very least, it is recommended that you take a course or training in interviewing skills. The interviewing process can be quite daunting if you are uncomfortable with the questions being asked, such as those questions with regard to Level 4 measures, isolation, and data conversion. Also, given that you work within an organization and your likely target is someone else working within that organization, there may be an intimidation factor that can prevent the respondent from providing data. A third party interviewer can often remove that intimidation factor.

Focus Groups. Focus groups are a great way to get important information from a group of people when dialog among the group is important. Focus groups work best when the topic on which participants are to focus is important to them. High quality focus groups and the questions that you ask produce discussions that address exactly the topics you want to hear about. The key to successful focus groups, however, is keeping the focus group focused. While focus groups are used for group discussion, a fair amount of planning goes into designing the protocol for the focus group. The conversations that transpire during the focus group are constructed conversations focusing on a key issue of interest. Table 3-5 presents a sample focus group protocol used to collect Level 3 data.

Action Plans. In some cases, action plans are incorporated into the WLP program. These action plans become part of the program in which participants complete the action plan prior to leaving the program. Action plans are used to collect Levels 3 and 4 data. When

Table 3-5. Focus group protocol for a study conducted on an emergency response support program.

Focus Group Facilitator Protocol

Purpose

This focus group is intended to help us understand how knowledge and skills gained in the program have been applied (Level 3).

During the focus group you will identify effectiveness with application, frequency of application, barriers, and enablers to application.

What to Do
1. Give yourself extra time.
2. Arrive a few minutes early to prepare the room.
3. Introduce yourself to the point of contact. Reinforce the purpose, and explain the process.
4. Set up the room so that the tables or chairs are in a U-shape so that participants can see each other and you can become part of the group.
5. Place tent cards at each seat.
6. As participants arrive, introduce yourself, give them refreshments, and chat a few minutes.
7. As you ask questions, your partner should write the answers, but not try to write every word. Listen for key issues. Listen for quotes that are meaningful and make important points that reinforce use of knowledge and skills.
8. When you have gathered the information you need, thank each person there. Clean up, thank your point of contact, and leave.
9. Find a place to debrief with your partner and clarify notes. Do it immediately, because you will surely forget something.
10. When you return, analyze the data.

What to Take
1. Map.
2. Point of contact telephone numbers.
3. Tent cards. Each tent card should have a number in a corner. Participants can write their first name just so you call them by name, but your notes will refer to the participant number.
4. Refreshments—something light, but a treat because people respond to food, and it relaxes the environment.
5. Flip chart.
6. Markers for the tent cards and the flip chart.
7. Focus group notepads.
8. An umbrella.

What to Wear

You will be in a comfortable environment, so ties and high-heels are not necessary, but do dress professionally. No jeans and tennis shoes: business casual.

What to Say

The intent is to understand how participants are applying what they learned during training. Start on time. You do not want to keep the participants over the allotted time.

1. Thank everyone for participating.
2. Introduce yourself and your partner. Tell them you are part of a research team conducting a study on the program. Reinforce with them that their input is important to this study. The results of the study will be used to improve training and other program support initiatives.
3. Share the purpose of the focus group.
4. Explain how the process will work and that their input is strictly confidential.
5. Have them put their first name on the tent card. Explain that the numbers in the corner of the tent card are for recording purposes and that in no way will their name be recorded. Explain that after the focus groups you and your partner will compile notes; your notes will be later compiled with those of the other focus groups. Also, tell them that their input in the focus group is supplemental to a question-naire that they may have already received.
6. Begin question 1 with participant 1.

Questions

Each person will answer each question before moving to the next question. The idea is to allow each person to hear what the others say so that they can reflect on their responses. We don't want "group think." We want to know what each individual thinks.

Q1. Now that you have had a chance to apply what you learned regarding your emergency response duties, how effectively have you been able to execute those duties?

Q2. What specific barriers have interfered with your ability to execute your duties?

Q3. What has supported your efforts?

Focus Group Note Pad

Question: _____

Notes	Notable Quotes

Date: _____

Location: _____   Page _____ of _____

Facilitator: _____

working with Level 3 data, the action plans are collected sometime after the program to see if the intended actions were executed. When working with Level 4 data, however, the action plan process becomes more comprehensive. Table 3-6 shows an action plan used to collect Levels 3 and 4 data. In section A, the participants include their name, objective, evaluation period, measure for improvement, current performance, and target performance. Identifying these measures prior to the program is an important step in securing credible follow-up data. During the program, participants are asked to complete sections B and C. Questions A, B, and C in section E are completed prior to the participant coming to the program.

Begin with question D in section E after the evaluation period ends; the participant will identify how much that measure actually changed during the last month of the evaluation period compared to the average before the training. The participant also explains the basis for this change. It is important that all claims of improvement and monetary benefit are supported to ensure credibility of any estimate that has been provided. Questions E, F, and G in section E are then completed. The last section, F, provides information about intangible benefits.

Basic Rule 3

Extreme data items and unsupported claims should not be used in ROI calculations.

Basic Rule 4

Estimates of improvements should be adjusted for the potential error of the estimate.

The action planning process should be an integral part of the WLP program, not an add-on or optional activity. To gain the maximum effectiveness from the use of action plans, the following steps should be considered:

▶ Communicate the action plan requirement early in the WLP process. One of the most negative reactions to the action planning process is when it comes as a surprise to participants. Prior to coming to the program, participants need to be aware of the expectations of the program and that the action planning process is part of it. When participants realize the benefits of the action planning

Table 3-6. Sample action plan for Levels 3 and 4 data.

A **Part I—Action Plan for the** ___Leadership 101___ ___Training Program___

Name: ___Medicine Gelatin Manager___ Instructor Signature: _____ Follow-Up Date: _____

Objective: ___Elimination of gelatin waste___ Evaluation Period: ___June 1___ to ___November 30___

Improvement Measure: ___Quality___ Current Performance: ___8,000 kg wasted monthly___ Target Performance: ___Reduce waste by 80%___

B

SPECIFIC STEPS: *I will do this*	END RESULT: *So that*
1. Take a more active role in daily gelatin schedule to ensure the manufacture and processing control of gelatin quantities.	1. Better control of gelatin production on a daily basis. This will eliminate the making of excess gelatin, which could be waste.
2. Inform supervisors and technicians on the value of gelatin and make them aware of waste.	2. Charts and graphs with dollar values of waste will be provided to give awareness and a better understanding of the true value of waste.
3. Be proactive to gelatin issues before they become a problem.	3. Able to make gelatin for encapsulation lines and making better decisions on the amounts.
4. Constantly monitor hours of encapsulation lines on all shifts to reduce downtime and eliminate the possibility of leftover batches.	4. Eliminate the excess manufacturing of gelatin mass and the probability of leftover medicine batches.
5. Provide constant feedback to all in the department, including encapsulation machine operators.	5. Elimination of unnecessary gelatin mass waste.

C

EXPECTED INTANGIBLE BENEFITS
Gelatin mass will decrease to a minimum over time, which will contribute to great financial gains for our company (material variance), which will put dollars into the bottom line.

(continued on page 60)

Table 3-6. Sample action plan for Levels 3 and 4 data (continued).

D Part II—Action Plan for the _____ **Leadership 101** _____ **Training Program**

Name: _____ Medicine Gelatin Manager _____ Objective: _____ Elimination of gelatin waste

Improvement Measure: _____ Quality _____ Current Performance: _____ 8,000 kg wasted monthly _____ Target Performance: _____ Reduce waste by 80%

E

ANALYSIS

A. What is the unit of measure? _____ Waste reduction _____ Does this measure reflect your performance alone? ☐ Yes ☑ No

If not, how many employees are represented in the measure? _____ 32

B. What is the value (cost) of one unit? _____ $3.60 per kg of gelatin mass

C. How did you arrive at this value? _____ This is the cost of raw materials and is the value we use for waste.

D. How much did this measure change during the last month of the evaluation period compared with the average before the training program?

(monthly value) _____ 2,000 kg monthly waste _____ Please explain the basis of this change and what you or your team did to cause it.
6,000 kg of waste eliminated. Reduction in machines from 19 to 12 created additional savings, but did not calculate. Gains in machine hours
(efficiency) in Encapsulation Department. More awareness of gelatin mass waste and its costs. Key contributing factors were problem-
solving skills, communicating with my supervisors and technicians and their willing response, and my ability to manage the results.

E. What level of confidence do you place on the above information? (100% = Certainty and 0% = No Confidence) _____ 70%

F. What percentage of this change was actually caused by the application of the skills from the _____ Leadership 101 _____ Training
Program? (0% to 100%) _____ 20%

G. If your measure is time savings, what percentage of the time saved was actually applied toward productive tasks? (0% to 100%) _____ N/A

F

ACTUAL INTANGIBLE BENEFITS

Gelatin mass waste has been a problem for our company since start-up; with low efficiency in the Encapsulation Department and the mistakes
made in the Gelatin Department, the waste was out of control. In the past few months, efficiency has increased, the Gelatin Department has
stabilized, and, as a result, waste is down considerably.

process and that the program is intended to improve key impact measures, they will take the program and the process more seriously.

▶ Describe the action planning process at the beginning of the program. While the action planning process was presented prior to participants attending the WLP program, it is important to reintroduce the evaluation process, including the action plan to the participants at the beginning of the first day of the program. This keeps the participants focused on the need to complete the action plan, as well as focused on the impact measures intended to improve, while they participate in the program.

▶ Teach the action planning process. An important prerequisite for action plan success is to understand how it works. Part of the program's agenda should be allocated to this process.

▶ Allow time to develop the plan. If the action planning process is an integrated part of the WLP program, time should be included during the course period to complete the action plan.

▶ Have the facilitator approve the action plan. It is imperative that the action plan be related to the program objectives and at the same time represent an important accomplishment for the organization when it is completed. It is helpful to have the facilitator fully engaged in the process and sign off on the action plan, ensuring that the plan reflects all of the requirements and is appropriate for the specific program. In some cases, a space is provided for the facilitator's signature on the action plan.

▶ Require participants to assign monetary value for improvement. This step allows participants the opportunity to contribute to the data conversion step that helps move you to Level 5, ROI. For this step to be effective, it may be helpful to provide examples of typical ways in which values can be assigned to actual data.

▶ Ask participants to isolate the effects of the program. Although the action plan itself is an issue because of the WLP program, improvements in the Level 4 measures will be influenced by other factors. While completing the action plan during the follow-up, participants are asked to estimate the improvement of their Level 4 measures that are related to the particular program.

▶ Ask participants to provide confidence levels for estimates. This step addresses the need to adjust for error in the estimation process.

- ▶ Require action plans to be presented to the group. Have participants present their action plans to help ensure that the process is thoroughly developed and encourage that actions are implemented on the job.
- ▶ Explain the follow-up mechanisms. Participants should leave the WLP program with a clear understanding of how the action plans will be followed. Some options for the follow-up process are
  - — Have the group reconvene to discuss progress on the plans.
  - — Have participants meet with their immediate managers and discuss success of the plan.
  - — The program evaluator, the participant, and the immediate manager meet to discuss the plans and information contained in it.
  - — Participants send the plans to the evaluator and discuss it on a conference call.
  - — Participants send the plans directly to the WLP department with no meetings or discussions. This option is most commonly used.
- ▶ Collect action plans at the predetermined follow-up time. It is critical to have an excellent response rate. Because the action planning process is built into the program, action plan response rates are typically very high.
- ▶ Summarize the data and calculate the ROI. Once all the action plans have been submitted, the data derived from the action plans, including the monetary benefits for the measures improved, is incorporated into the ROI equation.

While the action plan process can be quite successful, there are a couple of disadvantages. One is that the participant has no assurance of anonymity for information he or she provides, which may be somewhat biased and unreliable. Also, the action planning process can be somewhat time consuming for the participant and the supervisor. However, if both believe the program is important and that it is intended to improve critical measures in their work unit, the action planning process will be supported and can prove to be a valuable tool for the evaluation process.

Performance Records. Performance records are organizational records. Data found in performance records represents standard data used throughout the organization in reporting success for a variety of functions. It would be a wise investment of your time to learn what data is currently housed within your organization. You may find there is more available than you think.

Response Rates

An often-asked question when considering the data collection process is, "How many responses do you need to receive to make the data valid and useable?" The answer is, all of it! The typical approach to determining the response rate needed for a valid story of the success of a program and for valid results of an evaluation is to first consider the population and select the sample. The target sample often depends on the budget and the degree of confidence that the results of the sample can be inferred to the population.

In working with the ROI methodology, results are reported much more conservatively. This is done by reporting results only from those who provide data during the data collection process. This eliminates the inference to a larger population.

Say you have a program that you plan to implement that will include a population of 50 people. You will need responses from 48 people to ensure a 95% level of confidence using a sample size table. Guiding Principle #6 says that if no improvement data is available for a population or from a specific source, it is assumed that little or no improvement has occurred. Applying this principle means that for those people who do not respond to the data collection and who do not provide data, you will make no judgment with regard to their performance or to the impact the program made on business measures that they may have observed. Using this guiding principle as the standard, you are eliminating the issue of inferring to the larger population. In contrast to typical survey research, in which a small number of respondents is good enough, at a certain level of confidence, to infer that the results are applicable to the larger population, the ROI methodology makes no assumptions. Only the benefits reported by those who respond are considered—do not infer results to non-respondents. Therefore, it is critical that you get all of the data back.

Table 3-7 lists a variety of action items that can be taken to ensure an appropriate response rate. It all starts with providing advanced communication about the evaluation. No one likes to be hit with a detailed questionnaire unannounced. First, it only adds to participants' daily tasks; and second, some of the questions can be quite challenging if a heads up has not been given. Clearly communicate the reason for the evaluation and for the questionnaire. Participants need to understand that the evaluation is not about them, it is about improving the program. Identify those people who will see the results of the evaluation and ensure them that they will get a summary of the evaluation. Keep the questionnaire as brief as possible. Ask only those questions that are important to the evaluation. If you can afford it, have a third

Table 3-7. Actions to improve response rates for questionnaires.

Increasing Questionnaire Response Rates

- ☐ Provide advance communication about the questionnaire.
- ☐ Clearly communicate the reason for the questionnaire.
- ☐ Indicate who will see the results of the questionnaire.
- ☐ Show how the data will be integrated with other data.
- ☐ Let participants know what actions will be taken based on data.
- ☐ Keep the questionnaire simple and brief.
- ☐ Allow for responses to be anonymous—or at least confidential.
- ☐ Make it easy to respond; include a self-addressed, stamped envelope or return email address.
- ☐ If appropriate, let the target audience know that they are part of a carefully selected sample.
- ☐ Provide one or two follow-up reminders, using a different medium.
- ☐ Have the introduction letter signed by a top executive or administrator.
- ☐ Enclose a giveaway item with the questionnaire (pen, money, and so forth).
- ☐ Provide an incentive (or chance of incentive) for quick response.
- ☐ Send a summary of results to target audience.
- ☐ Distribute questionnaire to a captive audience.
- ☐ Consider an alternative distribution channel, such as email.
- ☐ Have a third party collect and analyze data.
- ☐ Communicate the time limit for submitting responses.
- ☐ Review the questionnaire at the end of the formal session.
- ☐ Allow for completion of the survey during normal work hours.
- ☐ Add emotional appeal.
- ☐ Design the questionnaire to attract attention, with a professional format.
- ☐ Provide options to respond (paper, email, Website).
- ☐ Use a local coordinator to help distribute and collect questionnaires.
- ☐ Frame questions so participants can respond appropriately and accurately.

Source: Phillips, J.J., editor. (1997). *Handbook of Training Evaluation and Measurement,* 3rd edition. Woburn. MA: Butterworth-Heinemann.

party collect and analyze the data so that participants feel comfortable that their responses will held in confidence and anonymity will remain.

Considerations When Selecting a Method

A first consideration when selecting a data collection method is the culture of the organization. How have other types of data collection been conducted in the past?

Think About This

Think about how you would manage the administration of a detailed, follow-up questionnaire. Table 3-8 is a data collection administration plan. There are three sections on the plan. The first section represents activities or actions you can take prior to the distribution of the questionnaire. The second section on the administrative plan represents actions that you can take during the evaluation process. The third section is for actions you can take after the evaluation process. Think about things that you can do that will help ensure you get a successful response rate to your data collection efforts and add them to the list.

Some organizations are averse to questionnaires. If this is the case, you may struggle with getting questionnaires back for your evaluation. Some organizations support data collection via questionnaire as along as it is automated. Consider the culture and use the method that best fits.

Along with organizational culture, there are additional issues that should be considered when selecting the data collection method. These are discussed in the following paragraphs.

Table 3-8. Data collection administrative plan.

Before the evaluation begins, we will

☐ Ask our senior executive to submit a letter announcing the importance of the evaluation.

☐

☐

☐

During the evaluation, we will

☐ Send a reminder one week after the questionnaire is administered.

☐

☐

☐

After the evaluation is complete, we will

☐ Send all respondents a summary copy of the results.

☐

☐

☐

Validity and Reliability. When selecting a data collection method, consider the technique that will give the most valid and reliable results. Bear in mind, you will have to balance accuracy with the cost of data collection. Only spend 5% to 10% of the fully loaded cost of the program on the evaluation. You don't want the evaluation to cost more than the program itself. All evaluation costs are included in the denominator of the ROI equation, further driving down the ROI percentage. But, you do want to take into consideration the technique and steps that will provide the best data.

A basic way to look at validity is to ask yourself, "Are you measuring what you intend to measure?" While validity assessment can be determined using sophisticated modeling approaches, the most basic approaches to determining the validity of the questions asked in an evaluation project is the use of your subject matter experts, as well as participants. The use of subject matter experts, along with additional resources, such as literature reviews and previous case studies, represents content validity. Do your questions match what other questions asked when measuring the same kind of program? Do your subject matter experts agree that the measures being taken represent the intended objectives of the program? Face validity, is simply answering the question: "Do the questions make sense to the participants?" A simple

Think About This

In a recent study of a state level capacity building program, the evaluators were asked to design a questionnaire to see if the volunteers of the program believed that the program was achieving its intended objectives. The evaluators asked the corporate office that was funding this program to sample a small number of participants to ensure that the questions were measuring what was intended to be measured and to ensure participants understood questions being asked. Rather than count on the participants to test the questionnaire, the corporate office ran the questionnaire up the ladder and all managers tied to the program said, "Yes, the questions represented the correct measures." However, when the questionnaire was distributed to the volunteers, the volunteers indicated that in no way did the questions represent what the program was intended to do.

Take care when developing your questionnaires to ensure that participants realize the intent of the program and that subject matter experts realize the actual application of the program.

sampling of potential participants to review the questionnaire can provide some indication that the questions are feasible.

While validity is concerned with whether you are measuring the right measures, reliability is concerned with whether respondents are consistent in their answers. The most basic test of reliability is repeatability. This is the ability to get the same data from several measurements made in the same way. A basic example of repeatability is administering the questionnaire to the same person repeatedly over a period of time. If the person responds the same way to the questions every time, there is minimum error, meaning there is high reliability. If, however, the participant randomly selected the answers, there would be high error, meaning there is low reliability.

Time and Cost. When selecting data collection methods, several issues should be considered with regard to time and cost. Consider the time required for participants to complete the instrument. Also, consider the time required for participants' supervisors to complete the instrument or coach the participants through the data collection process. Remember everything spent on data collection, including time for the completion of data collection instruments, is a cost to the program. Consider the overall cost of data collection, which includes printing costs and time to develop and test the questionnaire or whatever data collection instrument you plan to use. Consider the amount of disruption that the data collection will cause employees. Typically interviews and focus groups require the greatest disruption, however, they provide the best data. Balance the accuracy of the data you need to make a decision about the program with what it will cost you to get that data.

Utility. The last consideration when selecting a data collection method is utility. How useful will the data be, given the type of data you'll be collecting through the data collection process? Data collected through a questionnaire can be easily coded and put into a database and analyzed. With the help of automation, data generated through a questionnaire can quickly be summarized and the story of success be told. Data collected through focus groups and interviews, however, call for a more challenging approach to analysis. Though you often take those stories collected through dialogue with your respondents and summarize the story in your report, a better analysis of what your respondents are telling you can be conducted. This requires, however, developing themes for the data collected and coding those themes so that statistical analysis can be conducted. This type of analysis can be quite time consuming and, in some cases, frustrating if you do not immediately compile the data at the conclusion of the interview or the focus group. Although you often make mental notes during data collection of this type, you will quickly lose those notes if you don't record them in some structured way.

Another issue with regard to utility is, what can you do with the data? Consider whether you really need to ask a question in order to get the data to make a decision about the program. Remember, these are WLP programs. You are making business decisions about the programs; whether the programs are being offered through a corporate, government, nonprofit, community, or faith-based setting, you are still making business decisions about the program. How can you best allocate the resources that you're using to develop your people or improve your processes? With these issues in mind, think before asking a question. If you can't use the data, don't ask the question.

Defining the Source

Selecting the source of the data is critical in ensuring accurate data is collected. Sometimes it is necessary to go to multiple sources of data. A fundamental question should be answered when deciding on the source of the data:

Who (or what system) knows best about the measures you are taking?

The primary source of data is the participants. Who knows best about their perception of the course, what they learned, and how they are applying what they learned? Data sources for Levels 3, 4, and 5 include

- ▶ performance records
- ▶ participants
- ▶ participants' supervisors and managers
- ▶ participants' peers and direct reports
- ▶ senior managers and executives
- ▶ other sources.

Performance Records

Given the variety of sources for the data, one of the most credible data sources will be your organization or internal performance records. These records reflect performance in a work unit, department, division, region, or organization. Performance records can include all types of measures that are usually readily available throughout the organization. This is the preferred method of data collection for Level 4 evaluation, because it usually reflects business impact data. Keep in mind that sloppy record keeping may make locating valid data quite difficult.

Participants

Participants are the most widely used source of data for ROI analysis. They are always asked about their reaction to the program and participants are whom you assess to determine if learning has occurred. Participants are your primary source of data. They are the ones who know what they do with what they learned when they return to the job. They are the ones who know what happens that may prevent them from applying what they learned on the job. In addition, they are the ones who realize what impact their actions have on the job.

Although many people perceive participants as the most biased option, you have to keep in mind that people are typically honest. If you explain and reinforce to the participants that the evaluation is not about them, it is about the program, they can remove their personal feelings from their answers and provide unbiased data.

Participants' Supervisors and Managers

Supervisors and managers of the participants are another important source. In many situations, they have observed the participants as they attempt to use the knowledge and skills. Those managers, who are actively engaged in a learning process, will often serve as coaches to ensure that application does occur. In gathering data from the supervisors, you still have to keep in mind any potential bias that may occur.

Participants' Peers and Direct Reports

In evaluating at Level 3, participants' peers and subordinates are good sources of data, especially when you're implementing 360-degree feedback evaluation. Although gathering their input can increase the cost of the evaluation, their perspective may add a level of objectivity to the process.

Senior Managers and Executives

Senior managers and executives also provide valuable data, especially when you are collecting Level 4 data. Their input, however, is somewhat limited because they are removed from the actual application of the knowledge and skills applied. Senior managers and executives have been used in the data collection process when implementing a high profile, expensive leadership development program in which they have invested.

Other Sources

Internal and external experts, and external databases, provide a good source of data when you're trying to convert measures to monetary value. The ideal situation is to gather monetary value for the measures from the standard values that you currently monitor. Sometimes you have to resort to the experts, or the databases outside your own records.

Determining the Time of Data Collection

The last consideration in the data collection process is the timing of data collection. Typically, Level 1 data is collected at the end of the course, and Level 2 data is collected during the course, either at the end of the test, at the beginning when there is a pretest, or at the end as self-assessment questions on the exercises throughout the course.

Levels 3 and 4 data collection occurs sometime after the new performance has had a chance to occur—the time in which new behaviors are becoming routine. You do not want to wait until the new behavior becomes inherent and participants forget where they learned these new behaviors. Typically, Level 3 data collection occurs three to six months after the program, depending on the program. Some programs, in which skills should be applied immediately upon conclusion of the program, should be measured earlier—anywhere from 30 days to two months after the program. Level 4 data can be a little trickier, however.

While the ROI calculation is an annual benefit, do not wait a year to collect the Level 4 data. Senior executives won't wait; the problem will either go away, executives and senior managers will forget, or a decision will be made without the data. Collect the Level 4 measures either at the time of Level 3 data collection or soon after when impact has occurred. Then, annualize the improvement in the measure and convert to monetary benefits and include the value in the ROI calculation.

Getting It Done

In the previous chapter, you looked at developing objectives and you worked through the process of defining the measures of your program. Now, complete the data collection plan. Take the data collection plan from

Chapter 2 and complete it by filling out the data collection method you plan to use to collect your data at the various levels, the source(s) of your data, the timing for your data collection, and the person or team responsible for the data collection.

In the next chapter, you will learn to isolate the effects of the program from other influences that may have contributed to business impact.

4

Isolate Program Impact

■ ■

What's Inside This Chapter

This step in the ROI methodology attempts to delineate the direct contribution caused by the WLP program, isolating it from other influences. This chapter covers three critical areas:

► Understanding why this is a key issue
► Identifying the methods to do it
► Building credibility with a process.

Understanding Why This Is a Key Issue

Isolating the effects of a program on business impact data is one of the most challenging, yet necessary steps, in the ROI methodology. When addressed credibly, this step links learning directly to business impact.

Other Factors Are Always There

In almost every situation, multiple factors create business results. The world does not stand still while you conduct WLP programs. Many functions in the organization are attempting to improve the same metrics that are being influenced by WLP programs.

Think About This

You have conducted a sales training program to improve sales competencies for client relationship managers. This program is designed to increase sales as the managers use the competencies. Three months after the training, sales have increased. However, during the evaluation period, product marketing and promotion increased. Also, prices were lowered in two key product lines and new technologies enable the sales representatives to secure quotes faster, thus increasing efficiency and boosting sales. All of these factors influence sales. From the perspective of the sales training function, the challenge is to determine how much of the sales increase is due to the training. If a method is not implemented to show the contribution, then the WLP staff will lose credibility.

A situation where no other factors enter into the process would be almost impossible. Important arguments exist that support the need to take this step.

Without It, There Is No Business Link—Evidence Versus Proof

Without taking steps to show the contribution, there is no business linkage. There is only evidence that learning could have made a difference. Results have improved, although other factors may have influenced the data. The proof that the program has made a difference on the business comes from this step in the process—isolating the effects of the program.

Other Factors and Influences Have Protective Owners

The owners of the other processes influencing results are convinced that their processes made the difference. In the previous example, the marketing and advertising functions are probably convinced that the increase in sales is entirely due to their efforts. They present a compelling case to management, stressing their achievements. The IT department is also convinced that technology made the difference. They, likewise, can present a compelling case that technology implementation made the difference. In real situations, other processes, such as performance improvement, reward systems, and job redesign, have protective owners, and they often are very convincing that they made a difference.

To Do It Right—This Is Not Easy

The challenge of isolating the effects of the program on impact data is critical and can be done; but it is not easy for very complex programs, especially when strong-willed owners of other processes are involved. It takes a determination to address this situation every time an ROI study is conducted. Fortunately, a variety of approaches is available.

Without It—The Study Is Not Valid

Without addressing this issue, a study is not valid because there are almost always other factors in the mix and the direct connection to learning is not apparent. In every study, there are two things that you cannot do:

1. Take all the credit for the improvement without tackling the issue.
2. Do nothing, attempting to ignore the issue.

Both of these will lower the credibility of learning's connection to the business.

Myths About Isolating the Effects of the Program

Several myths about isolating the effects of the program often create concerns, confusion, and frustration with this process. Some researchers, WLP professionals, and consultants inflame this matter by suggesting that isolating the effects is not necessary. Here are the most common myths:

1. **Learning and development are complementary with other processes; therefore, you should not attempt to isolate the effects of learning**. Learning is complementary to other factors, all of which drive results. If a sponsor of a project needs to understand the relative contribution of WLP, this issue must be tackled. If accomplished properly, it will show how all the complementary factors are working together to drive the improvements.
2. **Other functions in the organization do not isolate the effects**. While some functions do not grapple with this issue because they try to make a convincing case that the improvement is related to their own processes, others are addressing the issue. A credible approach to address this issue is necessary. Notice the next time you complete a customer survey after you make a purchase or open a new account—do they ask you why you made the purchase? They are trying to isolate the results of multiple variables.

3. **If you cannot use a comparison group analysis (a research-based control group), then you should not attempt this step**. Although a comparison group analysis is the most credible approach, it will not apply in the vast majority of situations. Consequently, other methods must be used to isolate effects. The problem does not go away just because you cannot use your desired or favorite technique. The challenge is to find other processes that are effective and one that will work anytime, even if it is not as credible as the comparison group method.

4. **The stakeholders will understand the linkage; therefore, you do not need to attempt to isolate the effects of learning on impact measures**. Unfortunately, stakeholders see and understand what is presented to them. Absence of information makes it difficult for them to understand the linkage, particularly when others are claiming full credit for the improvement.

5. **Estimates of improvement provide no value**. The worst-case scenario is to tackle this issue with the use of estimates from those individuals who understand the process the most. Although this is a last choice position, it may provide value and be a credible process, particularly when the estimates are adjusted for the error of the estimate. Estimates are used routinely in other functions.

6. **Ignore the issue; maybe they won't think about it**. Unfortunately, audiences are becoming more sophisticated on this issue, and they are aware of multiple influences. If no attempt is made to isolate the effects of learning, the audience will assume that the other factors have had a tremendous effect, and maybe all the effect. Thus, credibility deteriorates.

These myths underscore the tremendous importance of tackling this issue. This is not to suggest that learning is not implemented in harmony with other processes. All groups should be working as a team to produce desired results. However, when funding is provided to different functions in the organization—with different process owners—there is always a struggle to show, and sometimes even to understand, the connection between what they do and the results. If you do not tackle this issue, others will—leaving WLP with less than desired budgets, resources, and respect.

Applying the Methods

With this clear understanding of the importance of isolating the effects of the program, applying the methods is the next challenge.

Getting Started

Before the specific methods are discussed, it is helpful to review two important principles. First, the chain of impact should be revisited. Although this step can be conducted on application data (separating the influence of other factors on the actual behavioral change), it is usually applied to impact data. This is the level where the concerns are raised. The amount of impact connected to the program is the key issue. After the impact data has been collected, the next step in the analysis is to isolate the effects of the program. This is the proof that learning made a difference.

Another important issue is to attempt to identify the other factors that have contributed to the improvement in the business results measures. This step recognizes that other factors are almost always present and that the credit for improvement is shared with other functions in the organization. Just taking this step is likely to gain respect from the management team.

Several potential sources can help identify these influencing factors. The sponsors of the project may be able to identify the factors. Subject matter experts, process owners, and those who are most familiar with the situation may be able to indicate what has changed to influence the results. In many situations, participants know what other factors have influenced their performance. After all, it is their direct performance that is being measured and monitored.

Basic Rule 5
At least one method must be used to isolate the effects of the solution.

By taking stock in this issue, all factors that contributed to improvement are revealed, indicating the seriousness of the issue and underscoring how difficult it is going to be to isolate the effects of the program.

Technique 1—Comparison Group Analysis

The most accurate and credible approach to isolate the effects of WLP programs is a comparison group analysis, known as the control group arrangement. This approach involves the use of an experimental group that attends the WLP program and a control group that does not. The composition of both groups should be as similar as possible, and, if feasible, the selection of participants for each group should be on a random basis. When this is possible and both groups are subjected to the same environmental influences, the differences in the performance of the two groups can be attributed to the training program. As illustrated in figure 4-1, the control group and experimental group do not necessarily have preprogram measurements. Measurements are taken after the program is implemented. The difference in the performance of the two groups shows the amount of improvement that is directly related to the training program.

Figure 4-1. Posttest only, control group design.

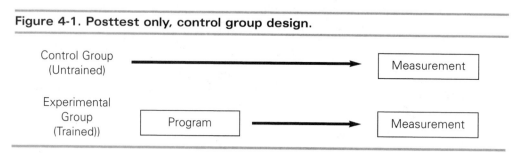

Assumptions. For the comparison group analysis to be used, five conditions must be met:

1. One or two outcome measures represent the consequence of the WLP program. This is the measure in question.
2. In addition to the WLP program, the factors that influence the outcome measures can be identified.
3. There are enough participants available from which to select the two groups.
4. The training can be withheld from the control group without any operational problems.
5. The same environmental influences affect both groups during the experiment (except that one group receives the training).

If these assumptions can be met, then there is a possibility for a control group arrangement.

Case Study. Retail Merchandise Company (RMC) is a large, national chain of 420 stores. The executives at RMC were concerned about the slow sales growth and were experimenting with several programs to boost sales. One of their concerns focused on the interaction with customers. Sales associates were not actively involved in the sales process, usually waiting for a customer to make a purchasing decision and then proceed with processing the sale. Several store managers had analyzed the situation to determine if more communication with the customer would boost sales. The analysis revealed that simple techniques to probe and guide the customer to a purchase should boost sales in each store.

The senior executives asked the WLP staff to experiment with a customer interactive skills program for a small group of sales associates. The training staff would prefer a program produced by an external supplier to avoid the cost of development, particularly if the program was not effective. The specific charge from the management team was to implement the program in three stores, monitor the results, and make recommendations.

The WLP staff selected the Interactive Selling Skills program, which makes significant use of skill practices. The program includes two days of training in which participants have an opportunity to practice each of the skills with a fellow classmate, followed by three weeks of on-the-job application. Then, in a final day of training, there is discussion of problems, issues, barriers, and concerns about using the skills. Additional practice and fine-tuning of skills take place in the final one-day session. At RMC, this program was tried in the electronics area of three stores, with 16 people trained in each store.

One of the most important parts of this evaluation is isolating the effects of the training program. This is a critical issue in the planning stage. The key question is, "When sales data is collected three months after the program is implemented, how much of the increase in sales, if any, is directly related to the program?" Although the improvement in sales may be linked to the WLP program, other non-training factors contribute to improvement. Though the cause-and-effect relationship between training and performance improvement can be very confusing and difficult to prove, it can be accomplished with an acceptable degree of accuracy. In the planning process, the challenge is to develop one or more specific strategies to isolate the effects of training and include it on the ROI analysis plan.

In this case study, the issue was relatively easy to address. Senior executives gave the training and development staff the freedom to select any stores for implementation of the pilot program. The performance of the three stores selected for the program was compared with the performance of three other stores that are identical in every way possible. This approach represents the most accurate way to isolate the effects of a program. Although other strategies, such as trend-line analysis and estimation, would also be feasible, the control group analysis was selected because the situation was appropriate and the analysis is very credible.

The challenge in the control group arrangement is to appropriately select both sets of stores.

Think About This

You have been tasked with developing the criteria to match the control and experimental groups in this case study. What are your criteria for matching the two groups?

- _____
- _____
- _____
- _____

It was important for those stores to be as identical as possible, so the WLP staff developed several criteria that could influence sales. This list became quite extensive and included market data, store level data, management and leadership data, and individual differences. In a conference call with regional managers, this list was pared down to the four most likely influences. The executives selected those influences that would count for at least 80% of the differences in weekly store sales per associate. These criteria were as follows:

- store size, with the larger stores commanding a higher performance level
- store location, using a market variable of median household income in the area where customers live
- customer traffic levels, which measures the flow of traffic through the store; this measure, originally developed for security purposes, provides an excellent indication of customer flow through the store
- previous store performance, a good predictor of future performance; the WLP staff collected six months of data for weekly sales per associate to identify the two groups.

These four criteria were used to select three stores for the pilot program and match them with three other stores. As a fallback position, in case the control group arrangement did not work, participant estimates were planned.

Problems With Comparison Groups. The control group process does have some inherent problems that may make it difficult to apply in practice. The first major problem is that the process is inappropriate for many situations. For some types of training programs, it is not proper to withhold training from one particular group while training is given to another. This is particularly important for critical skills that are needed immediately on the job. For example, in entry-level training, employees need basic skills to perform their job. It would be improper to withhold training from a group of new employees just so they can be compared to a group that receives the training. Although this would reveal the effect of initial training, it would be devastating to those individuals who are struggling to learn necessary skills, trying to cope with the job situation. In the previous case study, a control group is feasible. The training that was provided was not necessarily essential to the job, and the organization was not completely convinced that it would add value in terms of the actual sales.

This particular barrier keeps many control groups from being implemented. Management is not willing to withhold training in one area to see how it works in another. However, in practice, there are many opportunities for a natural control group arrangement to develop in situations where training is implemented throughout an organization. If it will take several months for everyone to receive the training, there may be enough time for a parallel comparison between the initial group being trained and the last group trained. In these cases, it is critical to ensure that the groups are matched as closely as possible, so the first two groups are very similar to the last two groups.

These naturally occurring control groups often exist in major WLP program implementations. The second problem is that the control groups must be addressed early enough to influence the implementation schedule so that similar groups can be used in the comparison. Dozens of factors can affect employee performance, some of them individual and others contextual. To tackle the issue on a practical basis, it is best to select three to five variables that will have the greatest influence on performance.

A third problem with the control group arrangement is contamination, which can occur when participants in the WLP program influence others in the control group. Sometimes the reverse situation occurs when members of the control group model the behavior from the trained group.

In either case, the experiment becomes contaminated because the influence of training filters to the control group. This can be minimized by ensuring that control groups and experimental groups are at different locations, have different shifts, or are

Noted

Your worst nightmare (with regard to experimental designs) is when the control group out-performs the experimental group.

on different floors in the same building. When this is not possible, it is sometimes helpful to explain to both groups that one group will receive training now and another will receive training at a later date. Also, it may be helpful to appeal to the sense of responsibility of those being trained and ask them not to share the information with others.

Closely related to the previous problem is the issue of time. The longer a control group and experimental group comparison operates, the greater the likelihood that other influences will affect the results. More variables will enter into the situation, contaminating the results. On the other end of the scale, there must be enough time so that a clear pattern can emerge between the two groups. Thus, the timing for control group comparisons must strike a delicate balance of waiting long enough for their performance differences to show, but not so long that the results become seriously contaminated.

A fifth problem occurs when the different groups function under different environmental influences. Because they may be in different locations, the groups may have different environmental influences. Sometimes the selection of the groups can help prevent this problem from occurring. Also, using more groups than necessary and discarding those with some environmental differences is another tactic.

A sixth problem with using control groups is that it may appear to be too research-oriented for most business organizations. For example, management may not want to take the time to experiment before proceeding with a program, or they may not want to withhold training from a group just to measure the impact of an experimental program. Because of this concern, some practitioners do not entertain the idea of using comparison groups. When the process is used, however, some organizations conduct it with pilot participants as the experimental group and non-participants as the control group. Under this arrangement, the control group is not informed of their control group status.

When implementing a control group to study a major ROI impact study, it is important for the program impact to be isolated to a high level of accuracy; the primary advantage of the control group process is accuracy.

Technique 2—Trend-Line Analysis and Forecasting

Another technique used to isolate the impact of WLP programs is the forecasting and trend-line analysis process. This approach has credibility if it is feasible and can be used, and it is a simpler alternative to the control group arrangement.

Trend-Line Analysis. A trend line is drawn using preprogram performance as a base and extending the trend into the future. After the program is conducted, actual performance is compared to the projected value, the trend line. Any improvement of performance over what the trend line predicted can then be reasonably attributed to training. For this to work, the following assumptions must be verified:

1. Preprogram data is available. This data represents the impact data—the proposed outcome of the training. At least six data points are needed.
2. Preprogram data should be stable, not very erratic.
3. The trend that has developed prior to the program is expected to continue if the program is not implemented to alter it.
4. No other new variables entered the process after the program was conducted. The key word is "new," realizing that the trend has been established because of the variables already in place, and no additional variables enter the process beyond the WLP program.

Case Study. In a warehouse where documents are shipped to fill consumer orders, shipment productivity is routinely monitored. For one particular team, the shipment productivity is well below where the organization desires it to be. The ideal productivity level is 100%, reflecting that the actual shipments equal the scheduled shipments.

Figure 4-2 shows the data before and after the team-training program. As shown in the figure, there was an upward trend on the data prior to conducting the training. Although the program apparently had a dramatic effect on shipment productivity, the trend line shows that improvement would have continued anyway, based on the trend that had been previously established. It is tempting to measure the improvement by comparing the average six-months shipments prior to the program (87.3%) to the actual average of six months after the program (94.4%), yielding a 7.1% difference. However, a more accurate comparison is the six-month actual average after the program compared to the trend line (92.3%); the difference is 2.1%. In this case, the conditions outlined above were met. Thus, using the lower measure increases the accuracy and credibility of the process to isolate the impact of the program.

Figure 4-2. Trend line of productivity.

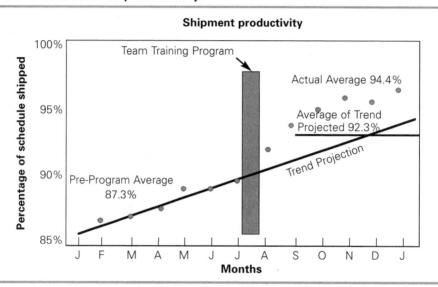

If the variance of the data is high, the stability of the trend line becomes an issue. If this is an extremely critical issue and the stability cannot be assessed from a direct plot of the data, more detailed statistical analyses can be used to determine if the data is stable enough to make the projection. The trend line can be projected with a simple routine available in many calculators and software packages.

Disadvantages and Advantages. A primary disadvantage of the trend-line approach is that it is not always accurate. The use of this approach assumes that the events that influenced the performance variable prior to the program are still in place after the program, except for the implementation of the training program. Also, it assumes that no new influences entered the situation at the time the training was conducted. This is seldom the case.

The primary advantage of this approach is that it is simple and inexpensive. If historical data is available, a trend line can quickly be drawn and differences estimated. Although not exact, it does provide a quick assessment of a training program's potential results.

Forecasting. A more analytical approach to trend-line analysis is the use of forecasting methods that predict a change in performance variables. This approach represents a mathematical interpretation of the trend-line analysis when other variables enter the situation at the time of training. The basic premise is that the actual performance of a measure, related to training, is compared to the forecasted value of that measure. The forecasted value is based on the other influences.

A major disadvantage with forecasting occurs when several variables enter the process. The complexity multiplies, and the use of sophisticated statistical packages for multiple-variable analyses is necessary. Even then, a good fit of the data to the model may not be possible. Unfortunately, some organizations have not developed mathematical relationships for output variables as a function of one or more inputs. Without them, the forecasting method is difficult to use.

The primary advantage of forecasting is that it can accurately predict business performance measures without training, if appropriate data and models are available.

Technique 3—Expert Estimation

An easily implemented method to isolate the effect of learning is to obtain information directly from experts who understand the business performance measures. The experts could be any number of individuals. Table 4-1 shows the potential expert sources. For many WLP programs, the participants are the experts. After all, their performance is in question and the measure is reflecting their individual performance. They may know more about the relationships between the different factors, including learning, than any other individual.

Because of the importance of estimations from program participants, much of the discussion in this section relates to how to collect this information directly from participants. The same methods would be used to collect data from others. The effectiveness of the approach rests on the assumption that participants are capable of determining how much of a performance improvement is related to the training program. Because their actions have produced the improvement, participants may have very accurate input on the issue. Although an estimate, this value will typically have

Table 4-1. Sources of input.

Expert Sources of Estimation
- Participants
- Supervisors
- Managers
- Sponsors
- Subject Matter Experts
- Process Owners
- External Experts
- Customers

credibility with management because participants are at the center of the change or improvement.

When using this technique, several assumptions are made:

1. A WLP program has been conducted with a variety of different activities, exercises, and learning opportunities, all focused on improving performance.
2. Business measures have been identified prior to the program and have been monitored following the program. Data monitoring has revealed an improvement in the business measure. (The process starts with this fact.)
3. There is a need to link the WLP program to the specific amount of performance improvement and develop the monetary effect of the improvement. This information forms the basis for calculating the actual ROI.
4. The participants are capable of providing knowledgeable input on the cause-and-effect relationship between the different factors, including learning and the output measure.

With these assumptions, the participants can pinpoint the actual results linked to the program and provide data necessary to develop the ROI. This can be accomplished by using a focus group or a questionnaire.

Focus Group Approach. The focus group works extremely well for this challenge if the group size is relatively small—in the eight to 12 range. If much larger, the groups should be divided into multiple groups. Focus groups provide the opportunity for members to share information equally, avoiding domination by any one individual. The process taps the input, creativity, and reactions of the entire group.

The meeting should take about one hour (slightly more if there are multiple factors affecting the results or there are multiple business measures). The facilitator should be neutral to the process (that is, the same individual conducting the program should not conduct this focus group).

The task is to link learning to business performance. The group is presented with the improvement, and they provide input on isolating the effects of learning. The following steps are recommended to arrive at the most credible value for learning impact:

1. **Explain the task**. The task of the focus group meeting is outlined. Participants should understand that there has been improvement in performance. While many factors could have contributed to the performance, the task of this group is to determine how much of the improvement is related to learning.

2. **Discuss the rules**. Each participant should be encouraged to provide input, limiting comments to two minutes per person for any specific issue. Comments are confidential and will not be linked to a specific individual.

3. **Explain the importance of the process**. The participant's role in the process is critical. Because it is their performance that has improved, the participants are in the best position to indicate what has caused this improvement; they are the experts in this determination. Without quality input, the contribution of learning (or any other processes) may never be known.

4. **Select the first measure and show the improvement**. Using actual data, show the level of performance prior to and following the program; in essence, the change in business results is reported. If the participants have individual data, the individual improvements should be used.

5. **Identify the different factors that have contributed to the performance**. Using input from experts and process owners—others who are knowledgeable about the improvements—identify the factors that have influenced the improvement (for example, the volume of work has changed, a new system has been implemented, or technology has been enhanced). If these are known, they are listed as the factors that may have contributed to the performance improvement.

6. **Identify other factors that have contributed to the performance**. In some situations, only the participants know other influencing factors, and those factors should surface at this time.

7. **Discuss the linkage**. Taking each factor one at a time, the participants individually describe the linkage between that factor and the business results using a time limit of two minutes. For example, for the learning influence, the participants would describe how the learning has driven the actual improvement by providing examples, anecdotes, and other supporting evidence. Participants may require some prompting to provide comments. If they cannot provide dialogue on this issue, there's a good chance that that factor had no influence.

8. **Repeat the process for each factor**. Each factor is explored until all the participants have discussed the linkage between all the factors and the business performance improvement. After this linkage has been discussed, the participants should have a clear understanding of the cause-and-effect relationship between the various factors and the business improvement.

9. **Allocate the improvement**. Participants are asked to allocate the percentage of improvement to each of the factors discussed. Participants are provided a pie chart that represents a total amount of improvement for the measure in question and are asked to carve up the pie, allocating the percentages to different improvements with a total of 100%. Some participants may feel uncertain with this process but should be encouraged to complete this step, using their best estimate. Uncertainty will be addressed later in the meeting.

10. **Provide a confidence estimate**. The participants are then asked to review the allocation percentages and, for each one, estimate their level of confidence in the allocation estimate. Using a scale of 0% to 100%, where 0% represents no confidence and 100% is certainty, participants express their level of certainty with their estimates in the previous step. A participant may be more comfortable with some factors than others, so the confidence estimate may vary. This confidence estimate serves as a vehicle to adjust results.

11. **Ask the participants to multiply the two percentages**. For example, if an individual has allocated 35% of the improvement to learning and is 80% confident, he or she would multiply 35% × 80%, which is 28%. In essence, the participant is suggesting that at least 28% of the business improvement is linked to the WLP program. The confidence estimate serves as a conservative discount factor, adjusting for the error of the

estimate. The pie charts with the calculations are collected without names, and the calculations are verified. Another option is to collect the pie charts and make the calculations for the participants.

12. **Report results**. If possible, the average of the adjusted values is developed and communicated to the group. Also, the summary of all of the information should be communicated to the participants as soon as possible.

Participants who do not provide information are excluded from the analysis. Table 4-2 illustrates this approach with an example of one participant's estimates. The participant allocates 50% of the improvement to the WLP program. The confidence percentage is a reflection of the error in the estimate. A 70% confidence level equates to a potential error range of ± 30% (100% × 70% = 30%). The 50% allocation to learning represents ± 15% (50% × 30%). Thus, the contribution could be 65% (50% + 15% = 65%) or 35% (50% × 15% = 35%) or somewhere in between. The participant's allocation is in the range of 35% to 65%. In essence, the confidence estimate frames this error range. To be conservative, the lower side of the range is used (35%).

This approach is equivalent to multiplying the factor estimate by the confidence percentage to develop a usable learning factor value of 35%. This adjusted percentage

Table 4-2. Example of a participant's estimation.

Factor That Influenced Improvement	Percentage of Improvement	Percentage of Confidence Expressed	Adjusted Percentage of Improvement
1. Learning Program	50%	70%	35%
2. Change in Procedures	10%	80%	8%
3. Adjustment in Standards	10%	50%	5%
4. Revision to Incentive Plan	20%	90%	18%
5. Increased Management Attention	10%	50%	5%
Total	**100%**		

Basic Rule 6
Estimates of improvement should be adjusted for the potential error of the estimate.

is then multiplied by the actual amount of the improvement (postprogram minus preprogram value) to isolate the portion attributed to the program. The adjusted improvement is now ready for conversion to monetary values and, ultimately, for use in developing the return on investment.

This approach provides a credible way to isolate the effects of the program when other methods will not work. It is often regarded as the low-cost solution to the problem because it takes only a few focus groups and a small amount of time to arrive at this conclusion. In most of these settings, the actual conversion to monetary value is not conducted by the group but developed in another way. For most data, the monetary value may already exist as a standard, acceptable value. However, if the participants must provide input on the value of the data, it can be approached in the same focus group meeting as another phase of the process in which the participants provide input into the actual monetary value of the unit. To reach an accepted value, the steps are very similar to the steps for isolation.

Questionnaire Approach. Sometimes focus groups are not available or are considered unacceptable for use in data collection. The participants may not be available for a group meeting, or the focus groups may become too expensive. In these situations, it may be helpful to collect similar information via a questionnaire. With this approach, participants address the same issues as those addressed in the focus group, but now on a series of impact questions imbedded into a follow-up questionnaire.

The questionnaire may focus solely on isolating the effects of learning, as detailed in the previous example, or it may focus on the monetary value derived from the program, with the isolation issue being only a part of the data collected. Using questionnaires is a more versatile approach when it is not certain exactly how participants will provide business impact data. In some programs, the precise measures that will be influenced by the program may not be known. This is sometimes the case in programs involving leadership, team building, communications, negotiations, problem solving, innovation, and other types of WLP initiatives. In these situations, it is helpful to obtain information from participants on a series of impact questions, showing how they have used what they have learned and how the work unit has been affected. It is important for participants to know about these questions before they receive the questionnaire. The surprise element can be disastrous in this type of data collection. The recommended series of questions is shown in table 4-3.

Table 4-3. Recommended series of questions for isolating program results.

1. How have you and your job changed as a result of attending this program (skills and knowledge application)?
2. What effects do these changes bring to your work or work unit?
3. How is this effect measured (specific measure)?
4. How much did this measure change after you participated in the program (monthly, weekly, or daily amount)?
5. What is the unit value of the measure?
6. What is the basis for this unit value? Please indicate the assumption made and the specific calculations you performed to arrive at the value.
7. What is the annual value of this change or improvement in the work unit (for the first year)?
8. Recognizing that many other factors influence output results in addition to learning, please identify the other factors that could have contributed to this performance.
9. What percentage of this improvement can be attributed directly to the application of skills and knowledge gained in the program? (0%-100%)
10. What confidence do you have in the above estimate and data, expressed as a percentage? (0% = no confidence; 100% = certainty)
11. What other individuals or groups could estimate this percentage or determine the amount?

Case Study. Perhaps an illustration of this process can reveal its effectiveness and acceptability. In a large global organization, the impact of a leadership program for new managers was being assessed. Because the decision to calculate the impact of learning was made after the program had been conducted, the control group arrangement was not feasible as a method to isolate the effects of training. Also, before the program was implemented, no specified business impact data was identified that was directly linked to the program. Participants may drive one or more of a dozen business performance measures. Consequently, it was not appropriate to use trend-line analysis. Participants' estimates proved to be the most useful way to assess the impact of the training on business performance. In a detailed follow-up questionnaire, participants were asked a variety of questions regarding the applications of what was learned from the program. As part of the program, the individuals were asked to develop action plans and implement them, although there was no specific follow-up plan needed.

Although this series of questions is challenging, when set up properly and presented to participants in an appropriate way, it can be very effective for collecting impact data. Table 4-4 shows a sample of the calculations from these questions for this particular program.

Although this is an estimate, the approach has considerable accuracy and credibility. Four adjustments are effectively used with this method to reflect a conservative approach:

1. The individuals who do not respond to the questionnaire or provide usable data on the questionnaire are assumed to have no improvements. This is probably an overstatement of results because some individuals will have improvements but not report them on the questionnaire. This is Guiding Principle #6.

Table 4-4. Sample of input from participants in a leadership program for new managers.

Participant Number	Annual Improvement Value	Basis for Value	Confidence	Isolation Factor	Adjusted Value
11	$36,000	Improvement in efficiency of group. $3,000 per month × 12 (group estimate)	85%	50%	$15,300
42	$90,000	Turnover reduction. Two turnover statistics per year. Base salary × 1.5 = 45,000	90%	40%	$32,400
74	$24,000	Improvement in customer response time (eight hours to six hours). Estimated value: $2,000 per month	60%	55%	$7,920
55	$2,000	5% improvement in my effectiveness ($40,500 × 5%)	75%	50%	$750
96	$10,000	Absenteeism reduction (50 absences per year × $200)	85%	75%	$6,375
117	$8,090	Team project completed 10 days ahead of schedule. Annual salaries $210,500 = $809 per day × 10 days	90%	45%	$3,276
118	$159,000	Under budget for the year by this amount	100%	30%	$47,700

Basic Rule 7

If no improvement data is available for a population or from a specific source, it is assumed that little or no improvement has occurred.

2. Extreme data and incomplete, unrealistic, and unsupported claims are omitted from the analysis, although they may be included in the intangible benefits.

Basic Rule 8

Extreme data items are unsupported claims and should not be used in ROI calculations.

3. Because only annualized values are used, it is assumed that there are no benefits from the program after the first year of implementation. In reality, leadership development should be expected to add value for several years after the program has been conducted.

Basic Rule 9

Only the first year of benefits should be used in the ROI analysis.

4. The confidence level, expressed as a percentage, is multiplied by the improvement value to reduce the amount of the improvement by the potential error. This is Guiding Principle #7.

When presented to senior management, the results of this study were perceived to be an understatement of the program's success. The data and the process were considered to be credible and accurate.

Collecting an adequate amount of quality data from the series of impact questions is the critical challenge with this process. Participants must be primed to provide data, and this can be accomplished in several ways.

1. Participants should know in advance that they are expected to provide this type of data along with an explanation of why the information is needed and how it will be used.
2. Ideally, participants should see a copy of this questionnaire and discuss it while they are involved in the program. If possible, a verbal commitment to provide the data should be obtained at that time.
3. Participants could be reminded of the requirement prior to the time to collect data. The reminder should come from others involved in the process—even the immediate manager.
4. Participants could be provided with examples of how the questionnaire can be completed, using likely scenarios and types of data.
5. The immediate manager could coach participants through the process.
6. The immediate manager could review and approve the data.

These steps help keep the data collection process with its chain of impact questions from being a surprise. It will also accomplish three critical tasks:

1. **The response rate will increase**. Because participants commit to provide data during the session, a greater percentage will respond.
2. **The quantity of data will improve**. Participants will understand the chain of impact and understand how data will be used. They will complete more questions.
3. **The quality of the data is enhanced**. With up-front expectations, there is greater understanding of the type of data needed and improved confidence in the data provided. Perhaps subconsciously, participants begin to think through consequences of training and specific results measures.

Participant estimation is a critical technique to isolate the effect of WLP; however, the process has some disadvantages. It is an estimate and, consequently, does not have the accuracy desired by some learning managers. Also, the input data may be unreliable because some participants are incapable of providing these types of estimates. They might not be aware of exactly which factors contributed to the results or they may be reluctant to provide data. If the questions come as a surprise, the data will be scarce.

Several advantages make this strategy attractive. It is a simple process, easily understood by most participants and by others who review evaluation data. It is inexpensive, takes very little time and analysis, and, thus, results in an efficient addition to the evaluation process. Estimates originate from a credible source—the individuals who produced the improvement.

The advantages seem to offset the disadvantages. Isolating the effects of learning will never be precise, but this estimate may be accurate enough for most clients and management groups. The process is appropriate when the participants are managers, supervisors, team leaders, sales associates, engineers, and other professional and technical employees.

This technique is the fallback isolation strategy for many types of programs. If nothing else works, this method is used. A fallback approach is needed if the effect of the learning must be isolated. The reluctance to use the process often rests with trainers, training managers, learning specialists, and performance improvement specialists. They are reluctant to use a technique that is not very precise. Estimates are typically avoided. However, the primary audience for the data (the sponsor or senior manager) will readily accept this approach. Living in an ambiguous world, they understand that estimates have to be made and may be the only way to approach this issue. They understand the challenge and appreciate the conservative approach, often commenting that the actual value is probably greater than the value presented. When organizations begin to use this routinely, it sometimes becomes the method of choice for isolation.

Data Collection From Other Experts. The previous approaches describe how data is collected from participants in the programs. Both the focus group approach and the questionnaire approach are helpful in collecting data from others. Sometimes the supervisor of program participants may be capable of providing input on the extent of training's role in performance improvement. In some settings, the participants' supervisors may be more familiar with the other factors influencing performance. Consequently, they may be better equipped to provide estimates of impact. A word of caution: If the supervisors are physically removed from the actual settings, it may be difficult for them to understand the impact of learning.

Sometimes even managers are asked to provide input, but only if they have some credible insight into the cause-and-effect relationship of these factors. If they are physically removed from the situation, they may not be very credible. Other possible sources of contributions include input from customers, external experts, the program sponsor, and any other group or individual who may be knowledgeable of these relationships.

Building Credibility With the Process
Several items regarding credibility must be addressed. This step in the ROI methodology is the most significant credibility issue.

Selecting the Techniques
Based on an analysis of best practice use of these techniques, table 4-5 shows the frequency with which these different techniques are used by over 200 organizations that have been applying the ROI methodology for five years or more. This table presents a high percentage level for comparison group analysis; the average use of this method in all impact studies would be significantly less. After all, these are the best practice organizations, and they have worked diligently to use the most credible analyses. The 20% representing "Other" is a variety of techniques that are less likely to be used.

With several techniques available to isolate the impact of learning, selecting the most appropriate techniques for the specific program can be difficult. Estimates are simple and inexpensive, while others are more time consuming and costly. When attempting to make the selection decision, several factors should be considered:

- feasibility of the technique
- accuracy provided with the technique, when compared to the accuracy needed
- credibility of the technique with the target audience
- specific cost to implement the technique
- the amount of disruption in normal work activities as the technique is implemented
- participant, staff, and management time needed with the particular technique.

Multiple Techniques
Multiple techniques or sources of data input should be considered because two sources are usually better than one. When multiple sources are used, a conservative method is recommended to combine the inputs. A conservative approach builds acceptance and credibility. The target audience should always be provided with explanations of the process and the various subjective factors involved. Multiple sources allow an organization to experiment with different techniques and build confidence with a particular technique. For example, if management is concerned about the accuracy of participants' estimates, a combination of a control group arrangement and participants' estimates could be attempted to check the accuracy of the estimation process.

Table 4-5. Best practice use of techniques.

Isolating the Effects of WLP Program

Method [1]	Best Practice Use [2]
1. Comparison Group Analysis	35%
2. Trend/Forecasting Analysis	20%
3. Expert Estimation	50%
4. Other	20%

1. Listed in order of credibility.
2. Percentages exceed 100%.

Credibility

It is not unusual for the ROI in WLP to be extremely large. Even when a portion of the improvement is allocated to other factors, the numbers are still impressive in many situations. The audience should understand that, although every effort was made to isolate the impact, it is still a figure that is not precise and may contain error. It represents the best estimate of the impact given the constraints, conditions, and resources available.

One way to strengthen the credibility of the ROI is to consider the different factors that influence the credibility of data. Table 4-6 is a listing of typical factors that influence the credibility of data presented to a particular group in the WLP setting. The particular issue of isolating the effects of the WLP program is influenced by several of these credibility factors. First, the representation of the source of the data is very critical. The most knowledgeable expert must provide input and be involved in the analysis in this topic. Also, the motives of the researchers can be a critical issue. A third party must facilitate any focus group that is done, and the data must be collected in an objective way. Also, the assumptions made in the analysis and the methodology of the study should be clearly defined so that the audience will understand the steps taken to increase the credibility. The type of data focuses directly on the impact data: The data has changed, and the challenge is to isolate the effects on that change. Managers prefer to deal with hard data, typically collected from the output of most programs. Finally, by isolating the effects of only one program, the scope of analysis is kept narrow, enhancing the credibility.

Table 4-6. The factors that influence the credibility of data.

- reputation of the source of the data
- reputation of the source of the study
- motives of the researchers
- personal bias of audience
- methodology of the study
- assumptions made in the analysis
- realism of the outcome data
- type of data
- scope of analysis

Getting It Done

In chapter 2, you were introduced to the data collection plan and the ROI analysis plan. Here is where you begin the ROI analysis plan.

Table 4-7 provides a blank ROI analysis plan. Transfer your Level 4 objectives to the first column of the ROI analysis plan. Then, identify the technique you will use to isolate the effects of the program from other influences, and write the techniques(s) in the second column aligned with each Level 4 measure. Remember, this step must be taken, so a technique should be included for each objective.

In the next chapter, you will continue completing the ROI analysis plan.

Table 4-7. ROI analysis plan.

Program: _____   Responsibility: _____   Date: _____

Data Items (Usually Level 4)	Methods for Isolating the Effects of the Program/ Process	Methods of Converting Data to Monetary Values	Cost Categories	Intangible Benefits	Communication Targets for Final Report	Other Influences/ Issues During Application	Comments

5

Do the Math

∎ ∎

What's Inside This Chapter

Here you will learn the basic steps involved in moving from Level 4 to Level 5, getting to the ROI calculation in only three steps:

▶ Converting data to monetary value
▶ Tabulating fully loaded costs
▶ Calculating the ROI.

Converting Data to Monetary Value

The fundamental difference between Level 4 and Level 5 begins with converting the benefits of the program (Level 4) to monetary value. For some, this is a frightening task; others recognize that if standard values for the measures are unavailable, there are techniques to get there.

Level 4 measures are defined as the consequence of applying knowledge and skills (Level 3) learned in a program. These consequences result in what is often categorized as hard data and soft data. But, what do these categories really mean?

Hard Data Versus Soft Data

Hard data typically meets the following criteria:

- easy to measure
- quantifiable
- easy to convert to monetary value
- objectively based
- common measures of organization performance
- immediately credible with management.

They are the primary measurements of improvement, presented in rational, undisputed facts and are easy to collect. Hard data is categorized as:

- output
- quality
- cost
- time.

Every organization, private, public, social, and academic, has some form of these measures. Table 5-1 provides examples of measures representing hard data. Although not all-inclusive, this list should cover some measures tracked by your organization.

Soft data represents measures that are

- difficult to measure
- difficult to quantify
- subjectively based
- less credible as performance measures
- behaviorally oriented.

The measures, although important, are often perceived as less reliable when measuring performance, due to an inherent level of subjectivity. Soft data is categorized as:

- work habits
- new skills
- climate
- development
- satisfaction
- initiative.

Table 5-1. Hard data.

Output	Quality
• Units Produced • Tons Manufactured • Items Assembled • Reports Processed • Students Graduated • Research Grants Awarded • Tasks Completed • Number of Shipments • New Accounts Generated	• Errors • Waste • Rejects • Rework • Shortages • Defects • Failures • Malicious Intrusions • Accidents
Cost	**Time**
• Budget Variances • Unit Costs • Variable Costs • Overhead Costs • Operating Costs • Penalties/Fines • Project Cost Savings • Accident Costs • Sales Expense	• Cycle Time • Response Time • Equipment Downtime • Overtime • Processing Time • Supervisory Time • Meeting Time • Work Stoppages • Order Response Time

Every organization has some measure that can be categorized as soft data. Table 5-2 presents measures of each category.

Think About This

Select whether you think the measure represents hard data or soft data.

Objective	Hard	Soft
1. Decrease error rates on reports by 20%.	☐	☐
2. Decrease the amount of time required to complete a project.	☐	☐
3. Increase the customer satisfaction index by 25% in three months.	☐	☐
4. Reduce litigation costs by 24%.	☐	☐
5. Improve teamwork.	☐	☐
6. Enhance creativity.	☐	☐
7. Increase the number of new patents.	☐	☐
8. Reduce absence.	☐	☐

Table 5-2. Soft data.

Work Habits	New Skills
• Absenteeism • Tardiness • First Aid Treatments • Safety Violations • Communication	• Decisions Made • Problems Solved • Grievances Resolved • Conflicts Avoided • Interaction with Staff
Climate	**Development**
• Number of Grievances • Employee Complaints • Employee Engagement • Organizational Commitment • Employee Turnover	• Number of Promotions • Number of Pay Increases • Requests for Transfer • Performance Appraisal Ratings • Job Effectiveness
Satisfaction	**Initiative**
• Job Satisfaction • Customer Satisfaction • Employee Loyalty • Increased Confidence	• Implementation of New Ideas • Innovation • Goals Achieved • Completion of Projects

Tangible Versus Intangible Data

Many of you probably considered measures like customer satisfaction, teamwork, creativity, and absence as your soft data items. But, think about this:

▶ If customer satisfaction is a soft measure, then how are quantitative values assigned to it to create a customer satisfaction index? Don't you place numbers on (or quantify) customer satisfaction?

▶ If executives apply their newly acquired leadership skills and you find that there is increased teamwork, why do you care? You hope it yields greater productivity leading to increased sales and reduced costs.

▶ Why do you care if your staff is more creative? Through the use of creative thinking, your product development meetings are more efficient.

▶ If absence is a soft measure, then how do you track it? Isn't someone keeping up with how many days you don't show up for work?

Ultimately, soft data leads to hard measures. Many people suggest that hard data represents tangible measures; others suggest that soft data represents intangibles.

Noted

Although there are five levels of data, intangible benefits represent the sixth type of data developed through the ROI methodology.

But, the idea of categorizing data as hard and soft is somewhat ambiguous. Tangible data should, therefore, be viewed as data you choose to convert to monetary value, and intangible data is data you choose not to convert.

All data can be converted to monetary value. As shown in figure 5-1, this is done by tying those soft measures to hard measures then converting the measure to either cost savings/avoidance or revenue converted to profit.

Though all measures can be converted to money, several factors should be considered. One factor is the cost to convert the measure. You don't want to spend more on data conversion than the evaluation itself. Importance of the measure is another consideration. Some measures, such as customer satisfaction and employee satisfaction, stand alone quite well. When that is the case, you might think twice before attempting to convert the measure to money. A third consideration is credibility. While most business decisions are made on somewhat subjective data, the source of the data, the perceived bias behind the data, and the motive in presenting the results are all concerns when data is somewhat questionable. Don't risk credibility just to calculate an ROI. Intangible measures of success may be where you stop.

Figure 5-1. Data conversion.

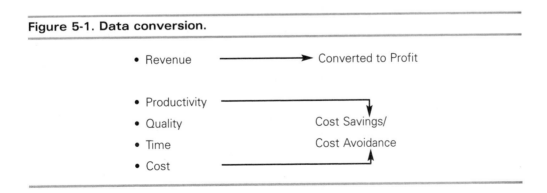

Think About This

Rank the following research results in order of credibility based on your definition of credibility. Have a colleague do the same, and discuss your rankings. Compare why you ranked the items as you did. Rank: 1 = least credible and 5 = most credible.

Rank

Study shows that brushing your teeth and rinsing with Listerine reduces plaque by 20%; compared to brushing and flossing alone, which reduces plaque only by 3.4%.
Source: *Wall Street Journal*, July 13, 2004.

_____

Vulcan Materials Company produced 195 million tons of crushed stone during 2001.
Source: Annual Report.

_____

Wachovia Bank receives 932% ROI in a training program for relationship managers.
Source: Phillips, P.P., editor. (2001). *Measuring Return on Investments. In Action Series*, volume 3. Alexandria, VA: ASTD.

_____

Survey based on in-home interviews shows a 5% decline in the number of 12-17 year olds who say they have ever used marijuana.
Source: *Wall Street Journal*, September 9, 2004.

_____

Verizon receives negative 85% ROI in a telephonic customer service skills program.
Source: Phillips, P.P., editor. (2001). *Measuring Return on Investments. In Action Series*, volume 3. Alexandria, VA: ASTD Press.

_____

Basic Rule 10

When collecting and analyzing data, use only the most credible sources.

Data Conversion Methods

There are variety of techniques available to convert a measure to monetary value. These are listed in table 5-3 in order of credibility. The success in converting data to monetary value is knowing what values are currently available. If values are not available, how best can you develop them? The first three techniques represent standard values.

Table 5-3. Techniques for data conversion.

- Using standard values
  — Output to contribution
  — Cost of quality
  — Employee's time
- Using historical costs
- Using internal and external experts
- Using data from external databases
- Linking with other measures
- Using estimations
  — Participants' estimates
  — Supervisors' and managers' estimates
  — WLP staff estimates

These are by far the most credible, because they are data that has been accepted by the organization. Following those, however, are the operational techniques to convert a measure to money.

Standard Values. Many organizations have standard values for measures of turnover, productivity, and quality. Those organizations that are involved in Six Sigma have a plethora of measures and along with them are the monetary values of those measures. Look around your organization. Talk to people and see what is being measured in other parts of the organization. Borrow from those other departments and functions. If a measure has had a monetary value developed and accepted by the organization, there is no reason for you to reinvent it. Take advantage of the work of others.

Standard values are grouped into three categories: output to contribution, cost of quality, and employees' time. When considering output to contribution, look at the value of an additional output. For example, organizations that work on a profit basis consider the marginal profit contribution in monetizing an additional sale. Think about Starbucks. The primary driver for customers coming to Starbucks is coffee. However, as you have noticed, there are cups, mugs, travel mugs, coffee grinders, and elaborate coffee pots, not to mention biscotti and chocolate. Along with those items, you often find bottled water, juices, and milk. What if, you, as store manager, find that these other items are not moving off the shelf as quickly as expected? You, along with other store managers, attend a one-week training to learn about these products and develop skills that will help you sell more products along with the coffee. Six months after the program, a comprehensive evaluation is conducted and you find that there has been an increase in sales in these peripheral products. The output is the increased sale. The contribution to the company, however, is the profit from the sale. Most organizations have a profit margin readily available.

Another example of converting output data to contribution is in looking at productivity measures. Those organizations that are performance driven rather than profit driven have a variety of data that represents productivity. The idea here is increasing the production or processing of one more item at no additional cost, thus saving the company money equivalent to the unit cost of processing or producing that item.

An example: At an academic institution, research grants are an important contribution to the funding of the university. You have limited staff within the office of research. Producing grant proposals has become a challenge. The office of research sends the staff to a report-writing training where staff members learn how to write grant proposals more effectively and efficiently. The time savings with this new efficiency will allow more grant proposals to be completed. Six months after the program, you find that the average weekly number of grant proposals completed has increased by five per week. This is the gain the university gets for producing an additional grant proposal. Just multiply that value by five and you calculate the weekly monetary gain. Based on the cost of developing a grant proposal, your institution has developed a standard value.

Look at one more example of output to contribution. Say you work at a passport office, and your entire role is to process passports. If you can process one more passport, given the resources and time you have available, the value of that one passport is equivalent to the cost of processing one passport. This one additional output—the passport—times the cost of processing the passport is the monetary contribution of increasing the output to the organization.

Now, look at the cost of quality, another standard value in organizations. Quality is a critical issue and its cost is an important measure in most manufacturing and service firms. Placing the monetary value on some measures of quality is quite easy. For example, waste, reject rates, and defects are often monitored in organizations and already have a monetary value placed on them. Other measures, such as re-work, can be converted to monetary value by looking at the cost of the work. For example, when employees make mistakes and errors in reporting, the cost of those mistakes—the value of those mistakes—is the cost incurred in re-working the report.

The third category of standard value is employees' time, probably the simplest and most basic approach to data conversion. If time is saved due to a program, the first question to ask is, "Whose time is it?" Then, to convert time to monetary value, take time saved times labor cost and add the percentage of additional value for employee benefits. This benefits factor can easily be obtained from the human resources department. A word of caution: When considering employee time as a benefit, the time savings is only realized when the amount of time saved is actually used for productive work. So, if a manager saves time by reducing the number of ineffective meetings the manager attends, the time saved should be applied to more work that is productive.

Think About This

What are the Level 4 measures you are trying to improve by implementing your program? Are standard values available for any of these measures?

Historical Costs. When no standard values exist, go to historical costs. The question is, "What has the incident cost in the past?" Using this technique often requires more time and effort than desired. In the end, however, you can develop a credible value for a given measure. This monetary value can eventually become a standard value.

An example of using historical costs is the case of a sexual harassment prevention program that was implemented in a large health care organization. The measure of the investigation was formal, internal complaints. The value of the complaint was determined by looking at the historical cost of a complaint. These historical costs included litigation complaints, legal fees and expenses, settlement losses, as well as investigation and defense of the organization. The cost of each of these was developed based on previous costs incurred by the organization for each complaint. Following the prevention program and at the end of the evaluation period, it was discovered that the organization had prevented 14.8 complaints due to the program. (This is after isolating other variables.) The monetary value for one complaint based on historical costs was then multiplied by the number of complaints reduced for the year due to the program.

Internal and External Experts. When standard values are unavailable and developing the monetary values through historical costs is not feasible, the next option is to go to internal or external experts. Using this approach, ask the expert to provide the cost for the value of one unit of improvement for the measure under investigation. Internal experts have knowledge of the situation and the respect of management. External experts are well published and have the respect of the larger community. In either case, keep in mind that these experts have their own methodologies to develop the values. Therefore, it's important for the experts to understand your intent and the measure for which you want to develop the monetary value. An example of using an internal expert to provide monetary value for a measure is in looking at the electric utility industry. All electric utility companies have on staff an expert in the development of rates. Typically, this expert is an economist. When a utility adjusts rates—raising and lowering rates—the monetary effect of that adjustment needs to be considered. This often falls to the economist. If rates were being manipulated, the executive staff calls the expert and asks for the estimate for the monetary value of the rate adjustment.

External Databases. Sometimes there is no a standard value and you don't have the resources to develop a monetary value using historical costs. You have no internal expert and can't find an external expert who can provide the information you seek. When this is the case, go to external databases. The Internet can provide you a wealth of information. No longer do you have to bury yourselves in libraries and dig through microfiche to uncover the research that has been conducted. External databases provide a variety of information, including the monetary value of an array of measures. An example of the use of external databases to convert a measure to monetary value is in the case of turnover. A company implemented a stress management program, which was driven by the excessive turnover due to the stress that came from changing a bureaucratic, sluggish organization into a competitive force in the marketplace. After implementing the stress management program, turnover was reduced along with improvements in other measures, such as productivity and job satisfaction. In calculating the ROI, the evaluators went to a variety of databases to determine the value of turnover for a particular employee's leaving the organization. The turnover studies used in the research revealed that a value of 85% of the annual base pay is what it was costing the organization for the people in this particular job classification to leave. While senior managers thought the cost of turnover was slightly overstated using the databases, it did give them a basis from which to begin determining the value of this particular measure.

Linking With Other Measures. When standard values, historical costs, and internal or external experts are not available and external databases don't provide the information that you need, another technique to convert a measure to monetary value is linking the value of that measure with other measures that have already been converted to monetary values. This approach involves identifying existing relationships showing a correlation between the measure under investigation and another measure to which a standard value has been applied. In some situations, the relationship between more than two measures is connected. Ultimately, this chain of measures is traced to a monetary value often based on profits. Keep in mind that the further you get from the actual monetary value, the greater the assumptions built in and the lower the credibility of the information. Using a methodology to link measures to other measures that have been converted to monetary value is often sufficient for converting measures when calculating the ROI of WLP programs.

Estimations. When the previous methods are inappropriate and you still want to convert a measure to monetary value, use an estimation process that has been proven conservative and credible with executives in a variety of organizations. The estimates of monetary value can come from participants, supervisors, managers, and even the WLP staff. The process of using estimation to convert a measure to monetary value is quite simple. The data can be gathered through focus groups, interviews, or questionnaires. The key is clearly defining the measure so that those who are asked to provide the estimate have a clear understanding of that measure.

The first step in the estimation approach is to determine who is the most credible source of the data. Typically, the participants realize the contribution they are making to the organization after participating in a WLP program. But, depending upon what job group those participants work in, you might develop data that is more credible if you go to the supervisors or managers. Only fall back on the WLP staff when you have no other option and are under pressure to come up with a monetary value. The concern with using WLP staff is the ownership that they have of the program, which increases bias and often results in loss of credibility, especially when reporting a very high ROI.

Consider the measure of absenteeism. You have an absenteeism problem, you implement a solution, and, as a result, the absenteeism problem is resolved. You now want to place a monetary value on an absence. You have no standard value. You don't want to invest the resources to develop a value using historical costs. There are no internal or external experts who can tell you. You've been unsuccessful in looking for an external database. You have no other measures that have been converted to monetary value to which you can link absenteeism. With pressure to come up with an ROI for this particular program, you decide to go to estimation.

The first step is determining who knows best what happened when an unexpected absence occurred. So, in an effort to convert the measure to monetary value, you call in five supervisors from similar work units to discuss the issue and help develop a value for an absence. Using a structured focus group approach, the scenario plays out as follows.

At the beginning of the focus group session, discuss the issue with the five supervisors, explaining why they have been brought together and that you are attempting to place a monetary value on an unexpected absence. Spend a few minutes in conversation about the issue before continuing the process. Then ask Supervisor One, "What happens when someone does not show up for work?" Supervisor One ponders the question for a moment and then says, "When someone doesn't show up for work, I have to call in a replacement. I hand the most pressing issues off to another employee who then has to interrupt her work to tend to the urgent tasks of the absent employee." Then go to Supervisors Two, Three, Four, and Five. Each supervisor takes about two minutes to tell what happens when someone doesn't show up for work.

The next step in the process is to have each supervisor estimate the monetary value or what it is costing the organization when unexpected absences and associated events occur. Ask Supervisor One, "Based on what you have told us about what occurs when someone does not show up for work, how much do you think one absence costs the organization per day?" Supervisor One considers her issues and all that occurs around an unexpected absence and says, "Based on what happens in my office when someone doesn't show up for work, I believe it costs us about $1,000 per day per absence." Write that down. Ask Supervisor Two the same question. Supervisor Two considers what Supervisor One said, but then she thinks about her own situation. She responds: "I understand where Supervisor One is coming from with her estimate, but given what happens in my department, I believe it costs more. I estimate it costs about $1,500 a day for an unexpected absence." Write that down. Ask the same question of Supervisors Three, Four, and Five and get their estimates. Now it's time to adjust for error.

Estimates are subjective, therefore, to reduce the error in the estimate, adjust for the supervisors' confidence. Start with Supervisor One saying, "You've told us what happens when someone doesn't show up for work. You estimate that it costs you $1,000 per day per unexpected absence. You've heard what happens in other supervisors' functions and how much they believe it's costing them when someone doesn't show up for work. Now, given what happens in your organization and your estimated costs and what you have heard from others, how confident are you that your estimate is accurate?" After thinking this over, Supervisor One says, "Well, it is an estimate, but I know what happens when people don't show up for work and I can be pretty sure what it's costing us from a time perspective. Given that it is an estimate and I'm not totally sure, I'll say that I am 70% confident in my estimate." Write that down. Repeat the process with Supervisor Two. Supervisor Two thinks about what she has said, what she has observed, and what she knows to be fact when someone doesn't show up for work. She considers what Supervisor One has said and the degree to which she adjusted her estimate. Supervisor Two says, "I'm probably high in my estimate. I feel fairly certain, but I'm probably not as sure as Supervisor One. I'm going to say that I'm 65% confident." Then repeat this part of the process with Supervisors Three, Four, and Five. In table 5-4, you see each supervisor's estimate of the per-day cost of one person not showing up for work, the confidence level in that estimate, and the adjusted per-day cost. Take the estimated per-day values, total them, and divide by the number of supervisors. This gives an average adjusted per-day cost for one absence of $1,061.

Figure 5-2 shows what happens when you adjust original estimates factoring for confidence level. The top line shows the original estimate for each supervisor. The bottom line shows the adjusted value. This additional step in the estimation process reduces variability in the estimates and provides a more conservative value. You have reduced the amount of error, hence, improved the reliability of the value of one absence.

Table 5-4. Absenteeism is converted using supervisor estimates.

Supervisor	Est. Per Day Cost	% Confidence	Adjusted Per Day Cost
1	$1,000	70%	$700
2	$1,500	65%	$975
3	$2,300	50%	$1,150
4	$2,000	60%	$1,200
5	$1,600	80%	$1,280
			$5,305
Average adjusted per-day cost of one absence			$1,061

Figure 5-2. Estimated value of absenteeism.

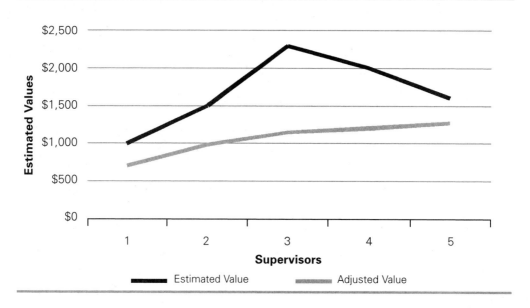

Data Conversion Four-Part Test

For those times when you cannot decide whether you can credibly convert a measure to monetary value, complete the four-part test:

1. If the measure you want to convert has a standard value, then convert it to monetary value.
2. If there is not a standard value, is there a method other than standard values to get there? If there is not a method, then report the measure as intangible.
3. If there is a method to convert the measure, can you do so with minimum resources? If no, then report it as intangible. (You don't want to spend more on data conversion than the evaluation itself.)
4. If you can convert the measure to monetary value using the selected method with minimum resources, can you convince your executive in two minutes or less that the value is credible? If no, then report the measure as intangible. If yes, then convert it!

Figure 5-3 presents the four-part test as a flowchart.

Figure 5-3. To convert or not to convert.

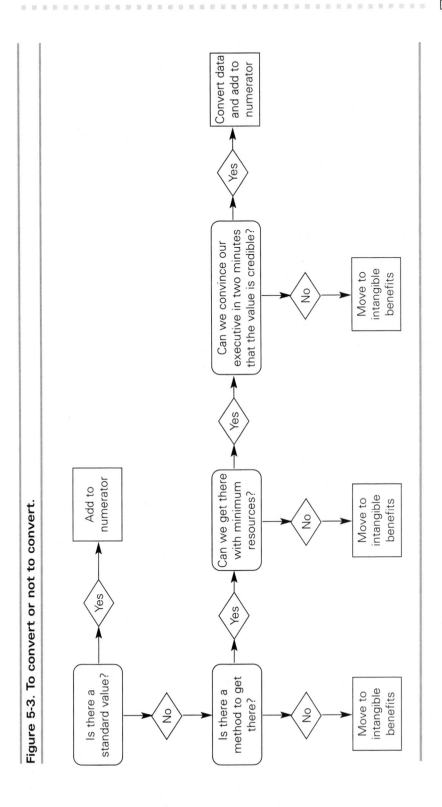

Basic Rule 11

In converting data to monetary value, when it doubt, leave it out!

Five Steps to Data Conversion

When you have decided to convert a measure to monetary value and chosen the technique that you're going to use to calculate the monetary value, then you are going to follow five steps to complete the data conversion process:

1. Focus on the unit of measure.
2. Determine the value of each unit.
3. Calculate the change in the performance of the measure.
4. Determine the annual improvement in the measure.
5. Calculate the total monetary value of the improvement.

Focus on the Unit of Measure. The first step is simply looking at one unit of the measure under investigation. If you are evaluating a measure of productivity and the output is one more credit card account, then your unit of measure is one credit card account.

Determine the Value of Each Unit. In determining the value of each unit, use standard values or one of the other operational techniques. In the credit card account example, you may find that one new account is worth $1,000. This figure is based on standard values using profit contribution. So, the value is $1,000 in profit.

Calculate the Change in the Performance of the Measure. Step 3 is actually taken during the evaluation process. Change in performance or the improvement in the number of credit card accounts is determined during the Level 4 evaluation. How many new credit card accounts did you achieve due to the program? Say that on average five new credit card accounts were established per month (after isolating all other factors).

Determine the Annual Improvement in the Measure. Annualize the improvement in the measure. Remember that Guiding Principle #9 says that for short-term programs you are going to report only first-year benefits. You are not going to wait one year to see exactly how many new credit card accounts you get due to the program. Rather, you're going to pick a point in time to get the average improvement to that date and, then, annualize that figure. In the credit card account example, you have the unit of measure as one account and the value of the unit is $1,000. You've established that the change in performance of the measure due to the program (after isolating the program) is averaging five new accounts per month. To determine the annual improvement in the measure, multiply the change in performance by 12 months. So, five per month times 12 months equals 60 new accounts due to the program.

Calculate the Total Monetary Value of the Improvement. Take the number from step 4, annual improvement in the measure (60 in the example), and multiply it by the value of each unit that you determined using the standard profit margin ($1,000 in the example). This gives you a total monetary value of improvement of $60,000. This is the value that goes in the numerator of the equation. Table 5-5 shows this calculation step-by-step.

$$BCR = \frac{\text{Program Benefits (\$60,000)}}{\text{Program Costs}}$$

$$ROI = \frac{(\text{Program Benefits [\$60,000]} \times \text{Program Costs})}{\text{Program Costs}} \times 100$$

Table 5-5. Five steps to data conversion.

Focus on the unit of measure
one credit card account

Determine the value of each unit
$1,000 profit per credit card account

Calculate the change in the performance of the measure
five new credit card accounts per month (after isolating other variables)

Determine the annual improvement in the measure
five accounts per month × 12 months = 60 new credit card accounts per year

Calculate the total monetary value of the improvement
60 per year × $1,000 per account = $60,000 annual value of the improvement

Basic Rule 12

Only the first year of benefits (annual) should be used in the ROI analysis of short-term solutions.

Now, you do it! Exercise 5-1 provides the information for each of the steps. All you have to do is complete steps 4 and 5. The answer to this exercise is found on page 124.

Tabulating Fully Loaded Costs

This next step in the move from Level 4 to Level 5 is tabulating the fully loaded cost of the program. When taking an evaluation to Level 4 only, this step is not necessary; although, regardless of how you evaluate your programs, it should be common practice to know the full costs of the WLP function and its various programs.

Exercise 5-1. Converting data to monetary values.

Scenario: Placing monetary value on grievance reduction

Step 1 **Focus on the unit of measure**
Our unit of measure is one grievance.

Step 2 **Determine the value of each unit**
The value of each unit is $6,500, as determined by internal experts.

Step 3 **Calculate the change in the performance of the measure**
The number of grievances declined by 10 per month; and after isolating the effects of the program, seven of the 10 fewer grievances were due to the program.

Step 4 **Determine the annual improvement in the measure**
The annual change in performance equals _____.

Step 5 **Calculate the total monetary value of the improvement**
The annual change in performance times the value equals _____.

The value that you put in step 5 is the value that goes in the numerator of the equation.

$$BCR = \frac{\text{Program Benefits (value from step 5)}}{\text{Program Costs}}$$

$$ROI = \frac{(\text{Program Benefits [value from step 5]} - \text{Program Costs})}{\text{Program Costs}} \times 100$$

So, what is meant by fully loaded costs? It means *everything*. In looking at table 5-6 of the four categories of costs, which category do you think includes the full cost of the program?

If you selected category D, you are right. The analysis and the development costs are prorated over the life of the program. Remember that, when you are conducting an ROI study; you don't necessarily conduct the study for all sessions of a program. Often you only pick one or two cohorts and conduct the study based on those offerings. The lifetime of the program is considered the time until a major program change occurs. If you are evaluating a program that will not change for one year and you offer the program 10 times during the year and you conduct an ROI study on one offering of that program, then your analysis costs and your development costs will be included only at the rate of one-tenth of the total of the analysis and development costs. Keep in mind that the other offerings are going to benefit from the investment in analysis and development as well. Program materials, instructor and facilitator costs, facilities costs, travel, lodging, meals, participant salary and benefits, and evaluation costs are expensed—they are the direct costs.

Overhead and administrative costs, however, are allocated based on the number of days of training for the program being evaluated. Table 5-7 provides an example. As you see in the table, the unallocated budget in the example is $548,061. To calculate the total number of participant-days, take the number of days for a program and multiply

Table 5-6. Cost categories.

Which Cost Category Is Appropriate for ROI?

A	B
Operating Costs Support Costs	Administrative Costs Participant Compensation and Facility Costs Classroom Costs
C	**D**
Program Development Costs Administrative Costs Classroom Costs Participant Costs	Analysis Costs Development Costs Delivery Costs Evaluation Costs Overhead and Administrative Costs

Table 5-7. Allocation of overhead and administrative costs.

Unallocated budget	$548,061
Total number of participant-days (five-day program offered 10 times a year - 50 participant days)	7400
Per-day unallocated budget ($548,061 ÷ 7400)	$74
Overhead and administrative costs allocated to a three-day training program (3 × $74)	$222

it by the number of times the program is offered (a five-day program offered 10 times a year equals 50 participant-days). In the example, there are 7,400 participant-days. The next step is to determine the per-day cost of the unallocated budget. The unallocated budget divided by the number of participant-days gives a per-day cost of $74 ($548,061 ÷ $7,400 = $74). The per-day costs are allocated to the number of days involved in the program being evaluated. If the program is a three-day training program, you would allocate $222 to overhead and administrative costs.

Basic Rule 13
When working in the denominator, when in doubt, leave it in.

Table 5-8 provides a worksheet to help you develop the fully loaded costs for your WLP programs.

Calculating the ROI

As explained in Chapter 1, ROI is reported in one of two ways: the benefit-cost ratio (BCR) or the ROI percentage. In simple terms, the BCR compares the economic benefits of the program with the cost of the program. A BCR of 2 to 1 says that for every $1 you invest, you get $2 back.

The ROI formula, however, is reported as a percentage. The ROI is developed by calculating the net program benefits divided by program costs times 100. A BCR of 2 to 1 translates into the ROI of 100%. This tells you that for every $1 you spend you get $1 back, after costs. Remember that you're working with net benefits and

Table 5-8. Cost estimating worksheet.

Analysis Costs	Total
Salaries and Employee Benefits—WLP Staff (No. of People × Average Salary × Employee Benefits Factor × No. of Hours on Project)	_____
Meals, Travel, and Incidental Expenses	_____
Office Supplies and Expenses	_____
Printing and Reproduction	_____
Outside Services	_____
Equipment Expenses	_____
Registration Fees	_____
Other Miscellaneous Expenses	_____
Total Analysis Cost	_____

Development Costs		Total
Salaries and Employee Benefits (No. of People × Avg. Salary × Employee Benefits Factor × No. of Hours on Project)		_____
Meals, Travel, and Incidental Expenses		_____
Office Supplies and Expenses		_____
Program Materials and Supplies		_____
Film	_____	
Videotape	_____	
Audiotapes	_____	
35mm Slides	_____	
Overhead Transparencies	_____	
Artwork	_____	
Manuals and Materials	_____	
Other	_____	
Printing and Reproduction		_____
Outside Services		_____
Equipment Expense		_____
Other Miscellaneous Expense		_____
Total Development Costs		_____

(continued on page 122)

Table 5-8. Cost estimating worksheet (continued).

Delivery Costs	Total
Participant Costs	_____
Salaries and Employee Benefits (No. of Participants × Avg. Salary × Employee Benefits Factor × Hrs. or Days of Training Time) _____	
Meals, Travel, and Accommodations (No. of Participants _____ × Avg. Daily Expenses × Days of Training)	
Program Materials and Supplies	_____
Participant Replacement Costs (if applicable)	_____
Lost Production (Explain Basis)	_____
Instructor Costs	_____
Salaries and Benefits _____	
Meals, Travel, and Incidental Expense _____	
Outside Services _____	
Facility Costs	_____
Facilities Rental	_____
Facilities Expense Allocation	_____
Equipment Expense	_____
Other Miscellaneous Expense	_____
Total Delivery Costs	=========

Evaluation Costs	Total
Salaries and Employee Benefits—WLP Staff (No. of People × Avg. Salary × Employee Benefits Factor × No. of Hours on Project)	_____
Meals, Travel, and Incidental Expense	_____
Participant Costs	_____
Office Supplies and Expense	_____
Printing and Reproduction	_____
Outside Services	_____
Equipment Expense	_____
Other Miscellaneous Expenses	_____
Total Evaluation Costs	=========
General Overhead Allocation	_____
TOTAL PROGRAM COSTS	=========

the ROI is reported as a percentage. The formula used here is essentially the same as ROI in other types of investments where the standard equation is annual earnings divided by investment.

There is one final equation to consider. This equation, also comparing monetary benefits to costs, is the payback period. While payback period is not ROI, it does provide an indication of whether a program will return its investment within a specific time period. The payback period equation is simply the BCR equation turned upside down. Take the program costs, the total investment of the program, and divide it by the benefits. An example: If the total investment in a program is $100,000, the estimated benefits are $200,000, and the payback period is six months.

$$\text{Payback Period} = \frac{\$100,000}{\$200,000} = 0.5 \times 12 \text{ months} = \text{six month payback period}$$

Remember that intangible benefits are those that you choose not to convert to monetary value. But, they are important and often more important than the actual ROI calculation. Typical intangible benefits that you do not convert to monetary value are job satisfaction, organizational commitment, teamwork, and customer satisfaction. You can convert these measures to monetary value; typically, however, when job satisfaction, organizational commitment, teamwork, and customer satisfaction are improved, you're satisfied enough with the improvement in these measures that the dollar value with that improvement is not relevant.

Getting It Done

You have completed almost all of the steps to the ROI methodology. Now, it's time to complete your ROI analysis plan. In chapter 4, you transferred your Level 4 measures to the ROI analysis plan; you selected techniques to isolate the effects of the program on the measure. Now, determine how you will convert these measures to monetary value. If your measure does not pass the four-part test, move the measure to the "Intangible Benefits" column. Identify the program costs that you plan to consider and those benefits that you plan to categorize as intangibles.

In the next chapter, you will look at the final step, but also one of the most important steps—communicating results. At that time you can complete the "Communication Targets" column in your ROI analysis plan.

Exercise 5-1. Answers to converting data to monetary values.

Scenario: Placing monetary value on grievance reduction

Step 1 **Focus on the unit of measure**

Our unit of measure is one grievance.

Step 2 **Determine the value of each unit**

The value of each unit is $6,500, as determined by internal experts.

Step 3 **Calculate the change in the performance of the measure**

The number of grievances declined by 10 per month; and after isolating the effects of the program, seven of the 10 fewer grievances were due to the program.

Step 4 **Determine the annual improvement in the measure**

The annual change in performance equals ___84___.

Step 5 **Calculate the total monetary value of the improvement**

The annual change in performance times the value equals $546,000 .

The value that you put in step 5 is the value that goes in the numerator of the equation.

$$BCR = \frac{\text{Program Benefits (546,000)}}{\text{Program Costs}}$$

$$ROI = \frac{(\text{Program Benefits [546,000]} - \text{Program Costs})}{\text{Program Costs}} \times 100$$

6

Toot Your Horn

■ ■

What's Inside This Chapter

This chapter presents the basics in communicating results of your ROI study, which includes:

▶ Targeting the message
▶ Developing reports
▶ Displaying data.

Targeting the Message

This final step in the ROI methodology is the most critical. Measurement and evaluation are worthless endeavors if the results of the evaluation are not communicated. You have to toot your own horn; no one else will. Besides, how else can you improve your programs and provide the necessary feedback to those interested in the outcomes of your programs? How can others understand the value programs contribute to the organization? Keep in mind, however, that communication is a sensitive issue. There are those who will support your efforts regardless of the story you tell. There are others, however, who are skeptical regardless of the story you tell. There are those who will form their opinions because of the story you tell and how you tell it. Different audiences need different information, and you need to present the information in a variety of ways to ensure that the message comes across appropriately.

The evaluation process generates data. In order to communicate the message found in this data properly, ask yourself three fundamental questions:

1. What do you need?
2. Whom do you ask?
3. How do you ask?

What Do You Need?

There are a variety of needs when communicating anything. Those needs range from getting approval for your programs to satisfying curiosity about what the WLP function is all about. Sometimes you are looking for additional support and affirmation for your efforts. You sometimes look for agreement that a change in a program needs to occur. You're often just interested in building credibility for your programs, thereby reporting results of your study to the general audience. Often you want to reinforce the need to make changes to the system to further support the transfer of learning. Sometimes you communicate results of your evaluations to prepare the WLP staff for changes in the organization or, better yet, to apprise the staff of opportunities to help them develop their skills.

Communication is often conducted to enhance the entire process as well as to emphasize a specific program's importance to the organization. The communication process is used to explain what is going on, why something might or might not have occurred, and the goals to improve a program when it results in a negative ROI. You can use the communication process to energize the WLP staff as well as senior management and supervisors about an upcoming program.

When a pilot program shows impressive results, use this opportunity to stimulate interest in continuing the program as well as stimulate interest for potential participants. Sometimes you use the communication process to demonstrate how tools, skills, or new knowledge can be applied to the organization. Table 6-1 provides a list of possible purposes to consider in determining why you want to communicate the process and the results.

Basic Rule 14

The results from the ROI methodology must be communicated to all key stakeholders.

Table 6-1. Checklist of needs for communicating results.

1. Needs Related to This Program
   - Demonstrate accountability for client expenditures.
   - Secure approval for a program.
   - Gain support for all WLP programs.
   - Enhance reinforcement of the program.
   - Enhance the results of future programs.
   - Show complete results of the program.
   - Explain a program's negative ROI.
   - Seek agreement for changes to a program.
   - Stimulate interest in upcoming WLP programs.
   - Encourage participation in WLP programs.
   - Market future WLP programs.

2. Needs Related to WLP Staff
   - Build credibility for the WLP staff.
   - Prepare the WLP staff for changes.
   - Provide opportunities for WLP to develop skills.

3. Needs Related to the Organization
   - Reinforce the need for system changes to support learning transfer.
   - Demonstrate how tools, skills, and knowledge add value to the organization.
   - Explain current processes.

Whom Do You Ask?

Once you identify your needs, the next step in targeting the message is to determine to whom you need to communicate results to satisfy your communication need. If you are communicating results so that you can secure approval for a new program, consider your client or the top executive as your target audience. If you are trying to gain support for a program, you might want to consider the immediate managers or team leaders of the targeted participant group. If you are interested in improving the immediate training process, including facilitation as well as the learning environment, target the WLP staff. If you want to demonstrate accountability for all WLP programs, then the target audience would be all employees in the organization. It is important to think through who can help you address and respond to your communication need. Some key questions that you want to ask when determining the most appropriate audience are

- Is the potential audience interested in the program?
- Does the potential audience really want to or need to receive this information?

> ► Has someone already made a commitment to this audience regarding communication?
> ► Is the timing right for this message to be presented to this audience?
> ► Is the potential audience familiar with the program?
> ► How does this audience prefer to have results communicated to them?
> ► Is the audience likely to find the results threatening?
> ► Which medium will be most convenient to the audience?

There are four primary audiences to whom you will always communicate the results of your ROI studies: the WLP team, participants, participants' supervisors, and clients.

WLP Team. The WLP team should receive constant communication of the results of all levels of evaluation. Levels 1 and 2 data should be reported to the WLP team immediately after the program. This provides them the opportunity to make adjustments to the program prior to the next offering. It also provides them information to consider when developing their professional development plan.

Participants. Participants are a critical source of data. Without participants, there is no data. Levels 1 and 2 data should always be reported back to participants immediately after the data has been analyzed. A summary copy of the final ROI study should also be provided to participants. In doing so, participants see that the data that they are providing to you is actually being used to make improvements to the program. This enhances the potential for additional and even better data in future evaluations. Also, following up with participants after you have made adjustments to a program reinforces that what participants tell you is important to the success of the WLP program and contributes value to the organization as a whole.

Participants' Supervisors. Your participants' supervisors are critical to the success of WLP programs. Without supervisors' support for a program, you will struggle to get participants engaged in the program and jeopardize the successful transfer of learning on the job when participants return to work. By reporting the ROI study results to the supervisors, you will clearly demonstrate to them that employees' participation in learning programs yields business improvement. Supervisors will see the importance of their own roles in supporting the learning process from program attendance to application.

Clients. The fourth group to whom you should always communicate the results of your ROI study is the client, the person or persons who fund the program. Here, it is important to report the full scope of success. The client wants to see the program impact on the business as well as the actual ROI. Although Levels 1 and 2 data are important to the client to some extent, it is unnecessary to report this data to the client immediately after the program. The client's greatest interest is in Levels 4 and 5 data. Providing the client a summary report for the comprehensive evaluations will ensure that the information clearly shows that programs are successful and, in the event of an unsuccessful program, that a plan is in place to take corrective action.

Think About This

Just like there are guiding principles to the ROI methodology, there are principles for communicating the results of an ROI study. The following list provides a broad view of these principles:

- Keep communication timely.
- Target communication to specific audiences.
- Carefully select communication media.
- Keep communication consistent with past practices.
- Incorporate testimonials from influential individuals.
- Consider the WLP function's reputation when developing the overall strategy.

How Do You Ask?

Consider the best means for asking what you need to ask. As in other steps in the ROI methodology, you have many options—meetings, internal publications, electronic media, program brochures, case studies, and formal reports. Your choice of media is important, especially in the early stages of implementing the ROI methodology. You want to make sure that you select the appropriate medium for the particular communication need and target audience.

Meetings. When considering meetings as the medium for communication, look at staff meetings and management meetings. When do the regularly scheduled meetings occur? By planning for communication during normal meeting hours, you are not disrupting your audiences' regular schedules. However, you do run the risk of having to wait to present your report until some future meeting when you can be added to the agenda. But, key players will be so interested in your ROI study that getting a slot on the earliest possible meeting agenda should not be a problem. Another meeting might consist of a discussion where you, a participant, and maybe a participant's supervisor sit on a panel to discuss a particular program. Panel discussions can also occur at regularly scheduled meetings or at a special meeting focused on the program. Best practice meetings are another opportunity to present the results of your programs. The meetings highlight the best practices in each function within the organization. A best practice meeting might mean presenting your ROI study at a large conference in a panel discussion, which includes WLP practitioners and managers from a variety of organizations. Business update meetings also present opportunities to provide information about your program.

Internal Publications. Internal publications are another way in which you can communicate to the employees. You can use these internal publications—newsletters, memos, break room bulletin boards—to report program progress and results as well as to generate interest in current and future programs. Internal hard copy communications are the perfect opportunity to recognize program participants who have provided data or responded promptly to your questionnaires. If you have offered incentives for participation in a program or for prompt responses to questionnaires, mention this in these publications. Use internal publications to tell human interest stories and highlight activities, actions, and encounters that occur during and as a result of the program. Be sure to accentuate the positive and announce compliments and congratulations generously.

Electronic Media. Electronic media, such as Websites, intranets, and group emailing, are emerging as important communication tools. These are often used to promote programs and processes being implemented in the organization. Take advantage of these opportunities to spread the word about the activities and successes of the WLP department. A word of caution: Use group emailing—whether organization-wide or to certain target audiences—sparingly, making sure that message content is solid and engagingly crafted.

Brochures. Program brochures are another way to promote WLP activities and offerings. Reporting results in a brochure that describes the program's process and highlights the program's successes can generate interest in your current program, stimulate interest in coming programs, and enhance respect and regard for the WLP function and staff.

Formal Reports. A final medium through which to report results is in the formal report. There are two types of reports—micro-level reports and macro-level scorecards—that are used to tell the success of WLP programs. Micro-level reports present the results of a specific program and include detailed reports, executive summaries, general audience reports, and single-page reports. Macro-level scorecards are an important tool in reporting the overall success of the WLP function.

Developing Reports

There are five types of reports to develop to communicate the results of the ROI studies. These include the detailed report, which is developed for every evaluation project; executive summary; general audience reports; single-page reports; and macro-level scorecard.

Detailed Reports

The detailed report is the comprehensive report that details the specifics of the program and the ROI study. This report is developed for every comprehensive evaluation that you conduct. It becomes your record and allows you the opportunity to replicate the study without having to repeat the entire planning process. By building on an existing study, you can save time, money, effort, and a great deal of frustration. The detailed report contains six major headings:

- need for the program
- need for the evaluation
- evaluation methodology
- results
- conclusions and next steps
- appendixes.

Need for the Program. Define and clarify the objectives for the program, making sure that the objectives reflect the five levels of evaluation. You should have objectives that relate to participant perspective, describe what participants are intended to learn, reflect how participants are intended to apply what they have learned, and reflect the outcomes that the knowledge and skills gained in this program will have on the organization. You will also present your target ROI and how you came to that particular target.

Need for the Evaluation. Typically, if the program is intended to influence Level 4 measures, this presents a need for evaluation. But, in some cases, it may be that the Level 4 measures were never developed so the intent of the evaluation is to understand the influence the program has had or is having on the organization. The intent of the evaluation may be to understand the extent to which the program successfully achieved the objectives. The need for the evaluation may be dependent upon the request of an executive. Clearly state the reasons in the report. Again, although this report will be distributed to key audiences, it is also the report that serves you and the WLP function both as the tool to refer to in future evaluations and to remind you what happened during this particular evaluation.

Evaluation Methodology. This clear, concise, and complete description of the evaluation process builds credibility for the results. You will provide an overview of the methodology. You will then describe each element of the process, including all options available at each step, which option(s) you chose, the reasons for your choice, all actions and activities related to each element of the process, and each step you took. For the data collection section of the report, you will spell out how you collected the data, why you collected the data that you collected, from whom you collected the data, why you collected the data from that particular source(s), when you collected the data, and why you settled on the data collection procedures that you did. You will also display a completed copy in detail of your data collection plan. You will then explain the ROI analysis procedures. Here, you will set out why you chose the method you chose to isolate the effects of the program. You will clearly state the myriad ways in which to isolate the effects of the program. Answer the question, "Why did you do what you did?" On data conversion, you are again going to explain how you developed the monetary values for the Level 4 impact measures linked to the program, again setting out the range of possibilities for data conversion. You will list those ways, and then you will clearly explain why you chose the techniques you chose. You will address the cost issue and provide the cost categories that you included in your ROI analysis. A word of caution: At this point, you will not include the actual cost of the program. Bear in mind that if you put the cost of the program in front of your audience too early, they will focus on the cost of the program and you will lose their attention. As with data collection, you will provide a detailed copy of the ROI analysis plan so that your audience can see a summary of exactly what you did.

Results. Now, it's time for your story—the results section, where the WLP program that has undergone this rigorous evaluation can shine! Here, you will provide the results for all levels of evaluation beginning with Level 1, Reaction, Satisfaction, and Planned Action. You will explain the intent for gathering reaction data, providing the specific questions the reaction data answers, and you will report the results. You will then move on to Level 2, Learning. You will explain why it's important to evaluate learning and the key questions that learning data answers. You will report the results. You will move on to Level 3, Application and Implementation. This is the greatest part of the story. Here, you will provide evidence that what was taught was used. You'll talk about how effectively knowledge and skills gained in the program have been applied by the participants and how frequently they have applied their new knowledge and skills. You'll talk about how the support system enabled participants to apply what they learned. Here, too, is where you will discuss barriers to the transfer of learning. It is important that you tell what happened. If the work environment did not support learning transfer, report that here. You will also explain that when you realized, through the evaluation process, that a problem was occurring and that the support system was not helping, you took action by going to talk to those who might know or who might provide information about how things could be changed to support the program next time.

Next, you'll discuss Level 4, Business Impact, including how the program positively influenced specific business outcomes. Here again, you'll reinforce the fact that you isolated the effects of the program to ensure that it is clear to your audience that you did take into account other influences that might have contributed to these outcomes. You'll describe your options for isolation and explain why you chose the option you chose.

Then, you'll report on Level 5, ROI. First, explain what is meant by ROI, clearly defining the ROI equation. Address the benefits of the program, the Level 4 measures, and how you achieved them. Explain how you converted data to monetary value; detail the monetary benefits of the program. Then, report the fully loaded costs of the program. Recall that earlier in the evaluation methodology section of the report you described the details of the cost items, but did not provide the dollar value. It is here, after monetary benefits are reported, where you set out the dollar values of the costs. The readers have already seen the benefits in dollar amounts; now give them the costs. If the benefits exceed the costs, then the pain of a very expensive program is relieved because the audience can clearly see that the benefits outweigh the costs. Finally, provide the ROI calculation.

The last part of the results section in the detailed report concerns intangible benefits. As you've learned throughout the book, intangible benefits are those items you choose not to convert to monetary value. You will again highlight those intangible benefits and the unplanned benefits that came about through the program. You will reinforce their importance and the value they represent.

Basic Rule 15
Hold reporting the actual ROI until the end of the results section.

Conclusions and Next Steps. Develop and report your conclusions based on the evaluation, answering these questions:

- ▸ Was the program successful?
- ▸ What needs to be improved?

Explain the next steps, clearly pointing out the next actions to be taken with regard to this program. Those actions could include continuing the program, adding new content, removing content, developing new job aids, converting some components from instructor-led facilitation to e-learning format, or developing a blended learning approach to reduce the training costs while maintaining the benefits you achieved from the program. You want to clearly identify the next steps and set out the dates by which these steps will be completed.

Appendixes. The appendixes include exhibits, detailed tables that could not feasibly be included in the text, and raw data (keeping the data items confidential). Again, the final report is a reference for you as well as a story of success for others.

Throughout your report, incorporate quotes—positive and negative—from respondents. Remember that there are ethical issues with regard to evaluation. It is tempting to leave out negative comments. However, you will enhance your credibility and gain respect for the WLP function if you tell the story as it is. By developing this detailed comprehensive report, you will have backup for anything that you say during a presentation. When conducting a future ROI study on a similar program, you will have your roadmap in front of you. Table 6-2 presents a sample outline of a detailed report.

Table 6-2. Impact study outline; detailed comprehensive report; 50–300 pages.

- General Information
  — Objectives of Study
  — Background
- Methodology for Impact Study ⎤
  — Levels of Evaluation
  — ROI Process   Builds
  — Collecting Data   credibility
  — Isolating the Effects of Training   for the
  — Converting Data to Monetary Values   process.
  — Costs
  — Assumptions (Guiding Principles) ⎦
- Results
  — General Information
    – Response Profile
    – Relevance of Materials
  — Participant Satisfaction ⎤
  — Learning
  — Application of Skills/Knowledge   The results with
  — Business Impact   six measures:
    – General Comments   Levels 1, 2, 3, 4, 5,
    – Linkage With Business Measures   and intangibles
  — ROI Calculation
  — Intangible Benefits ⎦
- Barriers and Enablers
  — Barriers
  — Enablers
  — Suggestions From Participants
- Conclusions and Recommendations
  — Conclusions
  — Recommendations
- Exhibits

Executive Summary

Another important report to develop is the executive summary. The executive summary follows the same outline as the detailed report although you leave out the appendixes and do not develop each section and subsection in such excruciating detail. You will clearly and concisely explain the need for the program, the need for the evaluation, and the evaluation methodology. Always include the methodology prior to the results. Why? When the reader understands and appreciates the methodology, the understanding and appreciation build credibility and respect for the results. Report the data from Level 1 through Level 5 and include the sixth measure of success—the intangible benefits. The executive summary is usually 10 to 15 pages in length.

General Audience Reports

General audience reports are a great way to describe the success of your programs to the employees. General audience reports may be published in organization publications, like newsletters or in-house magazines; reported in management and team meetings, where you briefly review the report in a meeting setting; and, finally, published as case studies. Case studies are published internally and externally. There are many opportunities to publish your story outside your organization, including trade or association publications or academic research publications. The key here is to tell the story to show that your programs are working and that, when they don't work, you are willing to take steps to improve the program.

Single-Page Reports

A final micro-level report is a single-page report. Table 6-3 shows an example of a single-page report. Single-page reports are used with great care. Do not report success of your program using the single-page report until you are sure that the audience understands the methodology. If an audience sees the ROI of a program without having an appreciation for the methodology used to arrive at the number, the audience will fixate on the ROI and never notice, much less form a regard for, information developed in the other levels of evaluation. Therefore, single-page reports are used with great care, but they are an easy way to communicate results to the appropriate audiences on a routine basis.

Macro-Level Scorecard

Macro-level scorecards can provide the results of the overall training process. Table 6-4 presents an example of a macro-level scorecard.

Table 6-3. Single-page report.

Sexual Harassment Prevention

- Level 1 Results—Participant Satisfaction
  - Overall rating of 4.11 out of a possible 5
  - 93% provided list of action items
- Level 2 Results—Learning
  - Posttest scores average 84
  - Pretest scores average 51
  - Improvement 65%
  - Participants demonstrated they could use skills successfully
- Level 3 Results—Application
  Survey distributed to a sample of 25% of participants (1,720)
  Response rate of 64% (1,102 returned)
  - 96% conducted meetings with employees and completed meeting record
  - On a survey of non-supervisory employees, significant behavior change was noted
    - 4.1 out of 5 scale
  - 68% of participants report that all action items were completed
  - 92% reported that some action items were completed
- Level 4 Results—Business Impact

Sexual Harassment Business Performance Measures	One Year Prior to Program	One Year After Program	Factor for Isolating the Effects of Program
Internal Complaints	55	35	74%
External Charges	24	14	62%
Litigated Complaints	10	6	51%
Legal Fees and Expenses	$632,000	$481,000	
Settlement/Losses	$450,000	$125,000	
Total Cost of Sexual Harassment Prevention, Investigation, and Defense	$1,655,000	$852,000	
Turnover (Non-Supervisory Annualized)	24.2%	19.9%	

- Level 5 Results—ROI
  - Total Annual Benefits $3,200,908
  - Total Costs $ 277,987
  - ROI   1,052%
- Intangible Benefits
  - Increased job satisfaction
  - Increased teamwork
  - Reduced stress

These scorecards provide a macro-level perspective of success and serve as a brief description of program evaluation as contrasted to the detailed report. They show the connection between the WLP program's contribution and the business objectives. The method of isolation is always included in the report to reinforce that you

Think About This

There are fundamental guidelines in reporting the results of the ROI results study to senior management. Two critical questions to consider prior to communicating with senior management are whether you will be believed if you have an extremely high ROI and whether senior managers can handle it if you have a negative ROI. With those two questions in mind, you need to consider the following guidelines:

- Plan a face-to-face meeting with senior managers (first one or two ROI studies).
- Hold results until the end of the presentation.
- Present the complete and balanced sets of measures beginning with Level 1.
- Emphasize the attributes of the methodology that ensure conservative results.
- Present a plan for program improvement.

For the first one or two ROI studies, present your detailed report during a regularly scheduled executive staff meeting. If senior executives know that you have an ROI study to present, they will make room for you on the agenda. Ask for one hour of their time. Present the study in painstaking detail. Have a copy of the comprehensive report for each senior manager available at the meeting. When you begin your presentation, be ready and have copies of your detailed report. Do not give the report out before your presentation. If you give them the report, they will be flipping through the pages to find the ROI calculation. Keep the stack beside you as you present your results. Present the results to the senior management team just as you have written the report: need for program, need for evaluation, evaluation methodology, results, conclusion, and next steps. Be thorough in reporting Levels 1 through 4, and do not fixate on or hurry to the ROI calculation—the entire chain of impact is important to reporting the success of the programs. Report Level 5, ROI, and the intangible benefits. Then, present your conclusions and next steps. At the end of your presentation, provide each senior manager a copy of your final report. Do you really expect the senior management team to read this detailed report? Certainly not. At best, they will give it to an assistant and have that assistant read the document and summarize the contents that you will have presented in the meeting. Why then go to the trouble of preparing this printed copy of the detailed final report for senior managers? To build trust. You've told them your story; now, all they have to do is look in the report to see that you covered the details and that you provided a thorough and accurate presentation of the report's contents.

After the first one or two studies, senior management will have bought into the ROI methodology. Of course, if you've worked the process well, they will have begun to learn the methodology long before your initial presentation. Given that, after the first or second study, you can start distributing the executive summary. Limit your report to senior management to the 10- to 15-page report. Again, it has all components, but not so many details.

After about five ROI studies, you can begin reporting to senior management using the single-page report. This will save time and money. Do remember, though, that the WLP staff will always have a copy of the detailed, comprehensive report.

Table 6-4. Macro-level scorecard.

Scorecard: Seven Categories of Data

0. Indicators	Number of Employees Involved
	Total Hours of Involvement
	Hours per Employee
	Training Investment as a Percentage of Payroll
	Cost per Participant
1. Reaction, Satisfaction, and Planned Action	Percentage of Programs Evaluated at This Level
	Ratings on Seven Items vs. Targets
	Percentage With Action Plans
	Percentage With ROI Forecast
2. Learning	Percentage of Programs Evaluated at This Level
	Types of Measurements
	Self-Assessment Ratings on Three Items vs. Targets
	Pre/Post—Average Differences
3. Application and Implementation	Percentage of Programs Evaluated at This Level
	Ratings on Three Items vs. Targets
	Percentage of Action Plans Complete
	Barriers (List of Top 10)
	Enablers (List of Top 10)
	Management Support Profile
4. Business Impact	Percent of Programs Evaluated at This Level
	Linkage With Business Measures (List of Top 10)
	Types of Measurement Techniques
	Types of Methods to Isolate the Effects of Programs
	Investment Perception
5. ROI	Percentage of Programs Evaluated at This Level
	ROI Summary for Each Study
	Methods of Converting Data to Monetary Value
	Fully Loaded Cost per Participant
Intangibles	Intangibles (List of Top 10)
	How Intangibles Were Captured

are taking steps to give credit where credit is due. The scorecard integrates a variety of types of data and demonstrates alignment among programs, strategic objectives, and operational goals.

Displaying Data

Data can be displayed in a variety of ways; the more comprehensive the display of data, the better the story is told within a limited space. Edward R. Tufte is one of the predominant leaders on the topic of graphical display of data. Tufte suggests that graphical displays of data should

- ▶ Show data.
- ▶ Induce the audience to think about the substance rather than the technology of the graphic production.
- ▶ Avoid distorting the story that the data has to tell.
- ▶ Present many numbers in a small space.
- ▶ Make large data sets coherent.
- ▶ Encourage the eye to compare different pieces of data.
- ▶ Reveal the data at several layers of detail from broad overview to fine structure.
- ▶ Serve a reasonably clear purpose: description, exploration, tabulation, or decoration.
- ▶ Be closely integrated with the statistical and verbal descriptions of a data set.

A general rule of Tufte's is to show many variables of data in one display. However, it is more important to understand the display and be able to clearly explain the contents of the display rather than provide a comprehensive depiction of your data, but stumble through the story.

Tables

Tables, often referred to as a matrices, are charts that have information arranged in rows and columns. They are simple to explain. They are great for summarizing data and provide one of the best ways to display numerical values. They assist the audience in understanding how the data is organized. They are also one of the most convenient ways of sorting and summarizing data for quick reference.

A basic table is shown in table 6-5. This simple frequency table shows the scores received on an exam in a four-week course. The first column represents the scores; the second column represents the frequency or the number of participants who scored that score; the next column represents the percent of the total number of participants scoring that particular score. The valid percent column (sometimes referred to as the adjusted percentage) is based on missing data (scores). In this example, there are no missing scores. So the valid percent and the percent columns are the same. The cumulative percent column shows the percentage of students who receive a certain score or less. For example, 72% of the participants scored 88 or less. This typical frequency table summarizes the test data.

Table 6-5. Frequency and percentage table.

Test Scores	Frequency	Percent[1]	Valid Percent[1]	Cumulative Percent
70	2	11.1	11.1	11.1
77	2	11.1	11.1	22.2
82	1	5.6	5.6	27.8
85	5	27.8	27.8	55.6
87	1	5.6	5.6	61.1
88	2	11.1	11.1	72.2
90	1	5.6	5.6	77.8
92	1	5.6	5.6	83.3
93	2	11.1	11.1	94.4
95	1	5.6	5.6	100.0
Total	18	100.0	100.0	

1. Percentages exceed 100%.

The next table is simply a one-way table. Table 6-6 shows two variables along the same axis. This means that two different variables are represented in columns. In the first column, you see variable 1, which is the participant's name. Variable 2 represents employment date. Both variables are presented in the columns of the table. This is most often used in summarizing data from evaluations.

Diagrams

Diagrams are charts made up primarily of geometric shapes, such as circles, rectangles, and triangles. Lines or arrows connect the shapes. They show how people, ideas, and things relate. Text is frequently included inside and outside these shapes to tell the story. Numerical values are sometimes used, though, to a lesser extent because diagrams generally display non-quantitative data. Flowcharts, critical path method

Table 6-6. One-way table.

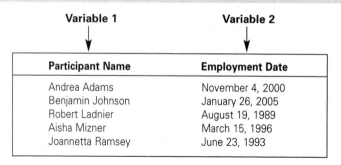

Participant Name	Employment Date
Andrea Adams	November 4, 2000
Benjamin Johnson	January 26, 2005
Robert Ladnier	August 19, 1989
Aisha Mizner	March 15, 1996
Joannetta Ramsey	June 23, 1993

charts, organization charts, network charts, decision charts, and conceptual charts are examples of data that are frequently presented in diagrams. The four-part test shown as a flowchart in figure 5-3 is an example of a diagram. Use diagrams to present project timelines, as well as the conceptual framework displaying the findings in an evaluation. Figure 6-1 represents a diagram displaying a phased approach to implementing a full-blown evaluation.

Figure 6-1. A phased approach to a comprehensive evaluation.

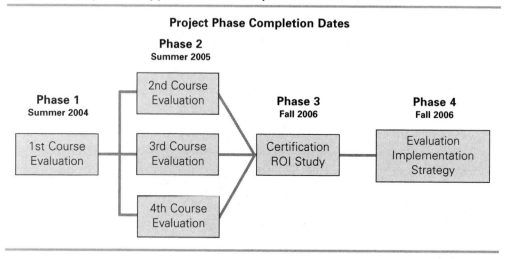

Figure 6-2 is another diagram displaying the argument for the conceptual framework discovered through the evaluation process. In this diagram, the course leads to positive reaction, knowledge acquisition, and the use of knowledge and skills. As a result, there is positive impact on network security, work stoppage, equipment downtime, uptime, and costs of troubleshooting. Through the isolation process, note the other variables that contribute to the Level 4 outcomes. Continuous learning and practice, research, real-world exercises, knowledge application, and reliable staff are listed and graphically depicted as influences on the outcomes. Providing a pictorial framework summarizes the results of the evaluation study in a manner that supports audience understanding.

Figure 6-2. Depiction of conceptual framework.

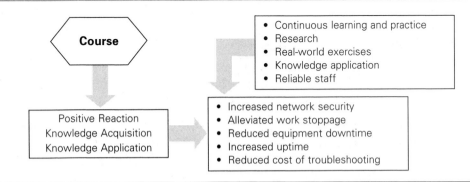

As participants react positively to the course, acquire knowledge and skills, and apply knowledge and skills, results occur. However, other intervening variables also influence measures; therefore, steps must be taken to isolate the effects of the course on these measures.

Graphs

Graphs are the most commonly used displays of quantitative relationships between two or more data types. Some types of graphs include bar charts, area graphs, line graphs, scatter graphs, histograms, box plots, and pie charts.

Histograms. Figure 6-3 is an example of a histogram. A histogram shows the frequency distribution of the data. As you see in this example, the scores of an exam taken by 60 participants in a training program are displayed. The mean score is 72.1 and the standard deviation is 12.0, which tells you that there was a wide variability among the scores. Also, in this histogram, the normal curve is plotted. This allows you to see at a glance whether the distribution of scores is skewed to the left or to the right. In beginning any analysis, the first step is to run the frequencies of the responses for the different measures and develop a frequency table as well as a histogram to examine the variability and the normalcy of the curve.

Figure 6-3. Histogram.

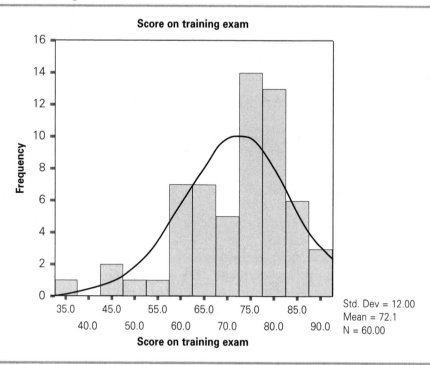

Score on training exam

Std. Dev = 12.00
Mean = 72.1
N = 60.00

Box Plots. Box plots provide a display of data comparing groups of data and how the results compare on a variety of measures. In figure 6-4, the box plot shows training exam scores for three groups. As you'll notice for group number one, the test scores range from approximately 45 to 85. The box represents interquartile containing 50% of the scores. The dark line in the middle of the box represents the median score that, in the case of group one, is 63.94. The standard deviation or the spread of scores is 13.5, which tells you there is a wide distribution of scores. Look at group two. The minimum score is not quite as low as in group one—47.56. The maximum score—89.65—is slightly higher than group one. The mean score is 73.57. The standard deviation for group two is 10.61, less variability. For group number three, the minimum score—71.77—is well above the minimum scores for the other two groups. The maximum score—89.69—is just slightly above the maximum score for group two. The median score is 80.19. The standard deviation for group three is only 4.41, making both the box and the line between the minimum and maximum

Figure 6-4. Box plot.

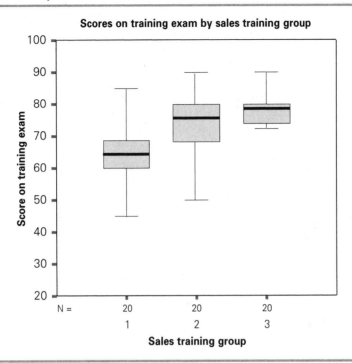

Scores on training exam by sales training group

smaller than for either of the other two groups. Using box plots you can clearly communicate the difference among groups.

Line Graphs. A line graph is a good way to display multiple variables and how they compare. The line graph in figure 6-5 compares data provided by three different sources—participants of a training course, the supervisors of the participants, and the customers of the participants. The example displays the extent to which each source of data expects participants to apply the knowledge and skills gained during a training course. As shown, the supervisors have a higher expectation of performance on determining performance gaps, defining root causes, and reconciling requests than either the participant or the customer. The customer, on the other hand, has the lowest expectations for defining root causes, managing implementation, troubleshooting implementation, and recommending the right solution. Line graphs provide a simple depiction when comparing data from multiple sources on a variety of measures.

Figure 6-5. Line graph.

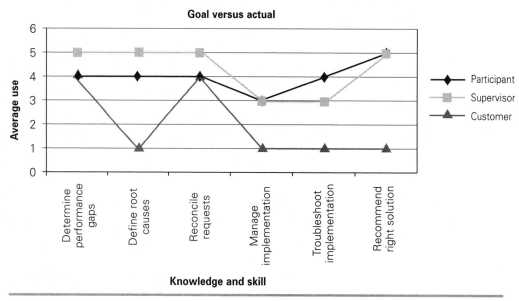

Source: Phillips, J.J., and P.P. Phillips. *ROI at Work*. Alexandria, VA: ASTD Press.

Graphical displays of data provide a concise reporting of results. They satisfy the need for those visual learners sitting at the executive table who may never hear a word you say, but who will respond to a picture!

Getting It Done

Now that you have read the final chapter on the ROI methodology, you have two actions you need to take. First, fill in the last two columns on the ROI analysis plan—"Communication Targets" and "Other Influences" (things that may affect the outcomes of the program or may affect the evaluation). Second, develop a communication plan, answering the following questions:

▸ What do you need from your communication? In answering this question, go back to the purpose of your evaluation. What are you trying to do? Improve the program? Ask for additional funding? Discontinue a program? Remember, there could be multiple needs.

▸ Whom do you ask? Who is the best audience for this communication? Remember that there are four key audiences to whom you will always communicate results. Is there another group with whom you need to communicate in order to address your need?

► How do you plan to ask? Are you going to set up a meeting or post something on the organization's intranet?

Your communication plan will have a variety of the reasons for the communication, audience whom you plan to address, and communication delivery methodologies.

In order to move forward with the content of this chapter, complete the communication plan in table 6-7. This will ensure that you develop the right reports, for the right purposes, targeting the right audiences, and using the most appropriate methods of distribution.

In the next chapter, make the ROI methodology routine while identifying and overcoming any barriers.

Table 6-7. Sample communication plan.

Need for Communication	Target Audience	Communication Document	Distribution Method

7

Sustain Momentum

■ ■

What's Inside This Chapter

Now that you know the basics of developing an ROI impact study, it's time to learn how to keep up the momentum. This includes:

▶ Identifying resistance to implementation
▶ Overcoming resistance to implementation
▶ Making the ROI methodology routine.

Identifying the Resistance

Resistance to comprehensive evaluation like the ROI methodology will be based on fear, lack of understanding, and an opposition to change and the efforts required to make a change successful.

Start With the WLP Team

The biggest resistance will probably come from within the WLP team. As Pogo, the famous cartoon character, once said, "We have met the enemy, and he is us." The staff may resist the extra efforts required to use ROI on the WLP process. The problems, concerns, or fears that arise must be uncovered and revealed.

Feedback from the WLP staff should be collected from formal meetings or questionnaires aimed at uncovering the particular areas of concern. What are the pressure points? What are the issues? What are the problems? They will quickly surface in this type of meeting or instrument. It is best to get all problems, concerns, and fears out in the open so that they can be addressed.

Also collect informal feedback from the individuals whose support is needed for the ROI process to work properly. Pay particular attention to those recognized as official or unofficial leaders. Formal assessment, feedback on concerns, and informal feedback expose many of the staff's issues with ROI. Table 7-1 shows typical statements of resistance.

Table 7-1. Typical objections to ROI.

1. This costs too much.
2. We don't need this.
3. This takes too much time.
4. Who is asking for this?
5. This is not in my job duties.
6. I did not have input on this.
7. I do not understand this.
8. Our clients will never buy this.
9. What happens when the results are negative?
10. How can we be consistent with this?
11. The ROI process is too subjective.
12. Our managers will not support this.
13. ROI is too narrowly focused.
14. This is not practical.

Some of these concerns are realistic; others are not. Implementing the ROI methodology will, no doubt, take additional effort and generate change in the way in which learning and development is implemented in the organization. This process will require making painful changes when programs are not living up to expectations. However, there are also many positive outcomes from this methodology. Yet, because of the concerns or fears, individuals may not be able to see the positive. For most implementations, many of the concerns about ROI are based on either lack of understanding or belief in the myths about ROI—a problem that can easily be confronted in a proper implementation process.

Next, Go to the Management Team

The management team will have questions about learning and development that must be analyzed and addressed. The first issue to recognize is that different levels of management have different concerns about the WLP process and ROI. Are the immediate managers of participants involved? If so, then their concerns should be addressed. Sometimes, the middle level of management, those who budget for WLP and support it in a variety of ways, may be the target. At other times, the concerns may come from top management where the ultimate commitment to WLP is crystallized. These are the individuals who must ultimately decide to what extent the WLP function will exist by providing the necessary resources and by supporting the process with highly visible actions.

Once the target is identified, the next step is to collect feedback. The instruments described earlier are appropriate for the management team as well. The responses can reveal much about management's perceptions of the success of the WLP process. The results quickly show concerns and areas where action is needed.

Others who are involved may have concerns that you should address. If there are outsourcing partners, input should be obtained from them as well. External groups, such as customer groups, involved with learning and development should also be included. The important issue is to make sure that those involved in supporting and sustaining the WLP process will have opportunities to sort out their concerns. Table 7-2 shows these groups' typical reactions to accountability issues and efforts. These reactions may be surprising to the WLP staff.

Now, Do a Gap Analysis

Given the concerns from the staff and various support and stakeholder groups, you should conduct a gap analysis. A gap analysis focuses on where things are compared to where they need to be. It may be helpful to conduct gap analyses in a variety of different areas as shown in table 7-3.

One of the most important issues is to assess the staff's capability for ROI. If there is a gap between actual versus needed knowledge and understanding of ROI, specific actions must be taken so that all individuals involved will be on track to use the methodology properly.

Another area that may need adjustment is the learning cycle. Evaluation must be considered early and often in the cycle. Data collection may need to be built into some processes, requiring participants and others to provide data as part of the learning process.

Table 7-2. Typical accountability reactions.

Accountability Issues
1. Is all of this training really needed?
2. How is learning and development helping our business?
3. Can we do this with less cost?
4. Do we have what it takes?
5. Why does this take so long?
6. Show me the money.

Reaction to ROI
1. Is this another one of your new jargons?
2. Is this the ROI that I know?
3. How can you do this?
4. Why didn't you do this earlier?
5. Is this credible?
6. Can we do this for every program?

Table 7-3. Typical gap categories.

1. Staff capability for ROI
2. Results-based learning process
3. Alignment with business needs
4. Effective policies, procedures, and templates
5. Appropriate environment for transfer of learning
6. Effective management support
7. The perception of value of learning

A third area of concern is business alignment—the extent to which programs are presently aligned to the business when compared to the best possible alignment. Often you must change practices and processes so that programs are more directly linked to business needs from the very beginning.

Policies, procedures, and guidelines often have to be changed so that evaluation becomes standardized, consistent, and routine. Policies and guidelines include statements about the percentage of programs that will be taken to various levels of evaluation, the extent of up-front business alignment with programs, and other important procedures.

Another important area to assess is the gap between reality and expectation in the workplace, which has to be analyzed and often changed to support the transfer of learning. In the initial analysis, the workplace must be free of barriers to learning transfer. Supporters and enablers should be in place to assist the transfer of learning from a program to on-the-job application. You should consider learning transfer issues before, during, and after programs are designed and implemented.

Next, management support is a key issue and specific efforts may be needed to improve support on different levels. To get managers involved, make sure they have the appropriate information and show them what the learning and development process is doing for them. A variety of support processes can make a difference in the success or failure of a program.

Finally, perceptions have to change—perceptions about the value of the WLP process and its contribution to the organization. Although the change may take time and require clear and wide-ranging evidence of success, it is necessary. With this gap analysis, the specific steps can be taken to narrow and close these gaps, so that you can overcome resistance to accountability efforts.

Overcoming Resistance to Implementation

To overcome resistance requires a methodical approach with a variety of actions, to remove or minimize or go around the barriers and problems identified in the gap analysis. When you overcome the resistance, you can accomplish implementation. Figure 7-1 shows the building blocks necessary to overcome the resistance to ROI implementation. The building blocks are approached from the first actions at the bottom of the figure to the last actions on the top so that each block can be put in place before moving to the next.

Identifying Roles and Responsibilities

A variety of roles and responsibilities are required if successful implementation is to be achieved. An important role is the ROI champion. This champion helps identify and delegate important responsibilities to ensure successful implementation.

Identifying a Champion. As a first step in the process, one or more individuals should be designated as the internal leader for ROI. As in most change efforts, someone must take the responsibility for ensuring that the process is implemented successfully. This ROI champion is usually the one who understands the process best and sees the vast potential for the contribution of the ROI methodology. This leader must be willing to teach and coach others. Table 7-4 presents the various roles of the ROI champion.

Figure 7-1. Building blocks for overcoming resistance.

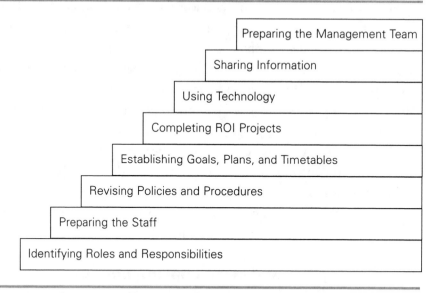

Table 7-4. Roles of the ROI champion.

Technical expert	Cheerleader
Consultant	Communicator
Problem solver	Process monitor
Initiator	Planner
Designer	Analyst
Developer	Interpreter
Coordinator	Teacher

The ROI leader is usually a member of the WLP staff who has this responsibility full time in larger organizations or part time in smaller organizations. The typical job title for a full time ROI leader is manager or leader of measurement and evaluation. Some organizations assign this responsibility to a team and empower them to lead the ROI effort.

Delegating Responsibilities to Ensure Success. Determining specific responsibilities is a critical issue because there can be confusion when individuals are unclear about their specific assignments in the ROI process. Responsibilities apply to two broad groups. The first is the measurement and evaluation responsibility for the entire WLP staff. This group is involved in designing, developing, delivering, coordinating, and supporting programs. Responsibilities include providing input on design of instruments, planning an evaluation, collecting data, and interpreting the results. Typical responsibilities include the following:

- ensuring that the needs assessment includes specific business results measures
- developing specific application objectives (Level 3) and business results objectives (Level 4) for each program
- focusing the content of the program on performance improvement— ensuring that exercises, tests, case studies, and skill practices relate to the desired objectives
- keeping participants focused on application and results objectives
- communicating rationale and reasons for evaluation
- assisting in follow-up activities to capture application and business results data
- providing assistance for data collection, data analysis, and reporting
- developing plans for data collection and analysis
- presenting evaluation data to a variety of groups
- assisting with the design of instruments.

Though it may be inappropriate to have each member of the staff involved in all of these activities, each individual should have at least one or more responsibilities as part of routine job duties. This assignment of responsibility keeps the ROI process from being disjointed and separate from major WLP activities. More important, it brings accountability to those who develop, deliver, and implement the programs.

The second issue involves the technical support function. Depending on the size of the WLP staff, it may be helpful to have technical experts provide assistance with the ROI methodology. When this group is established, it must be clear that the experts are there not to relieve others of evaluation responsibilities but to supplement technical expertise. Some firms have found this approach to be effective; and when this type of support is developed, responsibilities revolve around eight key areas:

- designing data-collection instruments
- providing assistance for developing an evaluation strategy
- coordinating a major evaluation project

- ▶ analyzing data, including specialized statistical analyses
- ▶ interpreting results and making specific recommendations
- ▶ developing an evaluation report or case study to communicate overall results
- ▶ presenting results to critical audiences
- ▶ providing technical support in any phase of the ROI process.

The assignment of responsibilities for evaluation is an issue that needs attention throughout the evaluation process. It is not unusual to require others in support functions to have responsibility for data collection. These responsibilities are defined when a particular evaluation strategy plan is developed and approved.

Preparing the Staff

Staff preparation is critical. Working with evaluation is a new endeavor for many leaders as well as WLP staff. For this reason, it is important for you to consider what knowledge, skills, and experiences the leaders and staff need to ensure successful implementation.

Developing the ROI Leaders. In preparation for the assignment to ROI leaders, individuals usually obtain special training to build specific skills and knowledge in the ROI methodology. The role of the implementation champion is very broad and serves a variety of specialized duties.

At times, the ROI implementation leader serves as technical expert, giving advice and making decisions about some of the issues involved in evaluation design, data analysis, and presentation. As an initiator, the leader identifies programs for ROI analysis and takes the lead in conducting a variety of ROI studies. When needed, the implementation leader is a cheerleader, bringing attention to the ROI methodology, encouraging others to become involved, and showing how value can be added to the organization. The implementation leader is also a communicator—letting others know about the process and communicating results to target audiences. All the roles can come into play at one time or another as the leader implements ROI in the organization.

Developing the Staff. A group that will often resist the ROI methodology is the staff who must design, develop, deliver, and coordinate WLP solutions. These staff members often see evaluation as an unnecessary intrusion into their responsibilities—absorbing precious time and stifling their freedom to be creative.

You should involve the staff on each key issue in the process. As policy statements are prepared and evaluation guidelines developed, staff input is absolutely essential. It is difficult for the staff to be critical of something they helped design, develop, and plan. Using meetings, brainstorming sessions, and task forces, the staff should be involved in every phase of developing the framework and supporting documents for ROI. In an ideal situation, the staff can learn the process in a two-day workshop and, at the same time, develop guidelines, policy, and application targets. This approach is very efficient, completing several tasks at the same time.

Using ROI as a Learning Tool—Not a Performance Evaluation Tool. One reason the staff may resist the ROI methodology is that the effectiveness of their programs will be fully exposed, placing their reputation on the line. They may have a fear of failure. To overcome this, the process should clearly be positioned as a tool for process improvement and not a tool to evaluate WLP staff performance, at least during its early years of implementation. WLP staff members will not be interested in developing a tool that will be used to expose their shortcomings and failures.

Evaluators can learn more from failures than from successes. If the program is not working, it is best to find this out quickly and understand the issues. If a program is ineffective, it will eventually be known to the clients and the management group, if they are not aware of it already. Lack of results will cause managers to become less supportive of WLP. Dwindling support appears in many forms, ranging from reducing budgets to refusing to let participants be involved in programs. If the weaknesses of programs are identified and adjustments are made quickly, not only will effective programs be developed, but also the credibility and respect for the function and the staff will be enhanced.

Revising Policies and Procedures

Another key part of implementation is revising the organization's policy concerning measurement and evaluation, often a part of policy and practice for developing and implementing WLP programs. The policy statement contains information developed specifically for the measurement and evaluation process. It is frequently developed with the input of the learning staff, key managers or sponsors, and the finance and accounting staff. Sometimes policy issues are addressed during internal workshops designed to build skills with measurement and evaluation. Table 7-5 shows the topics in the measurement and evaluation policy for a large organization.

Table 7-5. Results-based internal WLP policy.

1. Purpose.
2. Mission.
3. Evaluate all programs, which will include the following levels:
   a. Participant satisfaction (100%)
   b. Learning (no less than 70%)
   c. Job application (50%)
   d. Results (usually through sampling) (10%) (highly visible, expensive)
   e. ROI (5%).
4. Evaluation support group (corporate) will provide assistance and advice in measurement and evaluation, instrument design, data analysis, and evaluation strategy.
5. New programs are developed following logical steps beginning with needs analysis and ending with communicating results.
6. Evaluation instruments must be designed or selected to collect data for evaluation. They must be valid, reliable, economical, and subject to audit by evaluation support group.
7. Responsibility for WLP program results rests with trainers, participants, and supervisors of participants.
8. An adequate system for collecting and monitoring learning and development costs must be in place. All direct costs should be included.
9. At least annually, the management board will review the status and results of learning and development. The review will include plans, strategies, results, costs, priorities, and concerns.
10. Line management shares in the responsibility for learning programs evaluation through follow-up, pre-program commitments, and overall support.
11. Managers/supervisors must declare competence achieved through learning and development programs. When not applicable, the learning staff should evaluate.
12. External consultants must be selected based on previous evaluation data. A central data/resource base should exist.
13. All external programs of more than one day in duration will be subjected to evaluation procedures. In addition, participants will assess the quality of external programs.
14. WLP program results must be communicated to the appropriate target audience. As a minimum, this includes management (participants' supervisors), participants, and all learning staff.
15. Key WLP staff members should be qualified to do effective needs analysis and evaluation.
16. A central database for program development must be in place to prevent duplication and serve as program resource.
17. Union involvement is necessary in total WLP plan.

The policy statement addresses critical issues that will influence the effectiveness of the measurement and evaluation process. Typical topics include adopting the five-level ROI model presented in this book, requiring Levels 3 and 4 objectives in some or all programs, and defining responsibilities for learning and development.

Policy statements are very important because they provide guidance and direction for the staff and others who work closely with the ROI methodology. They keep the process clearly focused and enable the group to establish goals for evaluation.

Policy statements also provide an opportunity to communicate basic requirements and fundamental issues regarding performance and accountability. More than anything else, policy statements serve as a learning tool to teach others, especially when they are developed in a collaborative and collective way. If policy statements are developed in isolation and do not have the ownership of the staff and management, they will not be effective or useful.

Guidelines and processes for measurement and evaluation are important to show how to use the tools and techniques, guide the design process, provide consistency in the ROI methodology, ensure that appropriate methods are used, and place the proper emphasis on each of the areas. The guidelines are more technical than policy statements and often contain detailed procedures showing how the process is actually undertaken and developed. They often include specific forms, instruments, and tools necessary to facilitate the process.

Establishing Goals, Plans, and Timetable

As pointed out in chapter 2, planning is a critical part of the process—plan your work; work your plan. This rings true with taking steps to sustain your evaluation practice.

Setting Targets. Establishing specific targets for evaluation levels is an important way to make progress with measurement and evaluation. Targets enable the staff to focus on the improvements needed with specific evaluation levels. In this process, the percentage of programs planned for evaluation at each level is developed. The first step is to assess the present situation. The number of all programs, including repeated sections of a program, is tabulated along with the corresponding level(s) of evaluation presently conducted for each course. Next, the percentage of courses using Level 1 reaction questionnaires is calculated. The process is repeated for each level of the evaluation. The current percentages for Levels 3, 4, and 5 are usually low.

After detailing the current situation, the next step is to determine a realistic target for each level within a specific timeframe. Many organizations set annual targets for changes. This process should involve the input of the entire WLP staff to ensure that the targets are realistic and that the staff is committed to the process and targets. If the WLP staff does not develop ownership for this process, targets will not be met. The improvement targets must be achievable, while at the same time, challenging and motivating. Table 7-6 shows the annual targets initially established for the GAO.

Table 7-6. Evaluation targets for GAO.

Level of Evaluation	Percentage of Programs Evaluated at This Level
Level 1—Reaction	100%
Level 2—Learning	50%
Level 3—Job Application	30%
Level 4—Business Impact	10%
Level 5—ROI	5%

Using this example, 100% of the programs are measured at Level 1, which is consistent with many other organizations. Only half of the programs are measured at Level 2 using a formal method of measurement. At this level, informal methods are not counted as a learning measure. At Level 3, application represents a 30% follow-up. In essence, this means that almost one third of the programs will have some type of follow-up method implemented—at least for a small sample of those programs. Ten percent are planned for business impact and half of those for ROI. These percentages are typical and often recommended. The Level 2 measure may increase significantly in groups where there is much formal testing, or if informal measures (for example, self-assessment) are included as a learning measure. There is rarely a need to go beyond 10% and 5% for Levels 4 and 5. Sometimes these annual targets are set with multiple year goals to reflect the gradual improvement of increasing evaluation activity at Levels 3, 4, and 5.

Target setting is a critical implementation issue. It should be completed early in the process with full support of the entire learning staff. Also, if practical and feasible, the targets should have the approval of the key management staff, particularly the senior management team.

Think About This

What percentage of your programs do you evaluate at each level?

Level 1	_____ %
Level 2	_____ %
Level 3	_____ %
Level 4	_____ %
Level 5	_____ %

Developing a Project Plan. An important part of the planning process is to establish timetables for the complete implementation process. The timetables become a master plan for the completion of the different elements, beginning with assigning responsibilities and concluding with meeting the targets previously described. Figure 7-2 shows an ROI implementation project plan for a large petroleum company.

From a practical basis, this schedule is a project plan for transition from the present situation to a desired future situation. The more detailed the document, the more useful it will become. The project plan is a living, long-range document that should be reviewed frequently and adjusted as necessary. More important, it should always be familiar to those who are routinely working with the ROI methodology.

Completing ROI Projects

The next major step is to complete the ROI projects undertaken initially. A small number of projects are usually initiated, perhaps two or three programs. The selected programs usually represent the functional areas of the business, such as operations, sales, finance, engineering, and information systems. It is important to select a manageable number so the projects will be completed.

Ultimately, the number of programs tackled depends on the resources available to conduct the studies, as well as the internal need for accountability. Using the profile GAO uses, for an organization with 200 programs, this means that 5% (10) of the programs will have ROI results studies conducted annually, and at least 30% (60) will have some type of follow-up (Level 3).

As the projects are developed and the ROI implementation is under way, status meetings should be conducted to report progress and discuss critical issues with appropriate team members. For example, if a leadership program is selected as one of the ROI projects, all of the key staff involved in the program (design, development, and delivery) should meet regularly to discuss the status of the project. This keeps the project team focused on the critical issues, generates the best ideas to tackle particular problems and barriers, and builds a knowledge base to implement evaluation in future programs.

These meetings serve three major purposes: reporting progress, learning, and planning. The meeting usually begins with a status report on each ROI project, describing what has been accomplished since the previous meeting. Next, discussions take place about the specific barriers and problems encountered. During the discussions, new issues are interjected in terms of possible tactics, techniques, or

Figure 7-2. ROI implementation project plan for a large petroleum company.

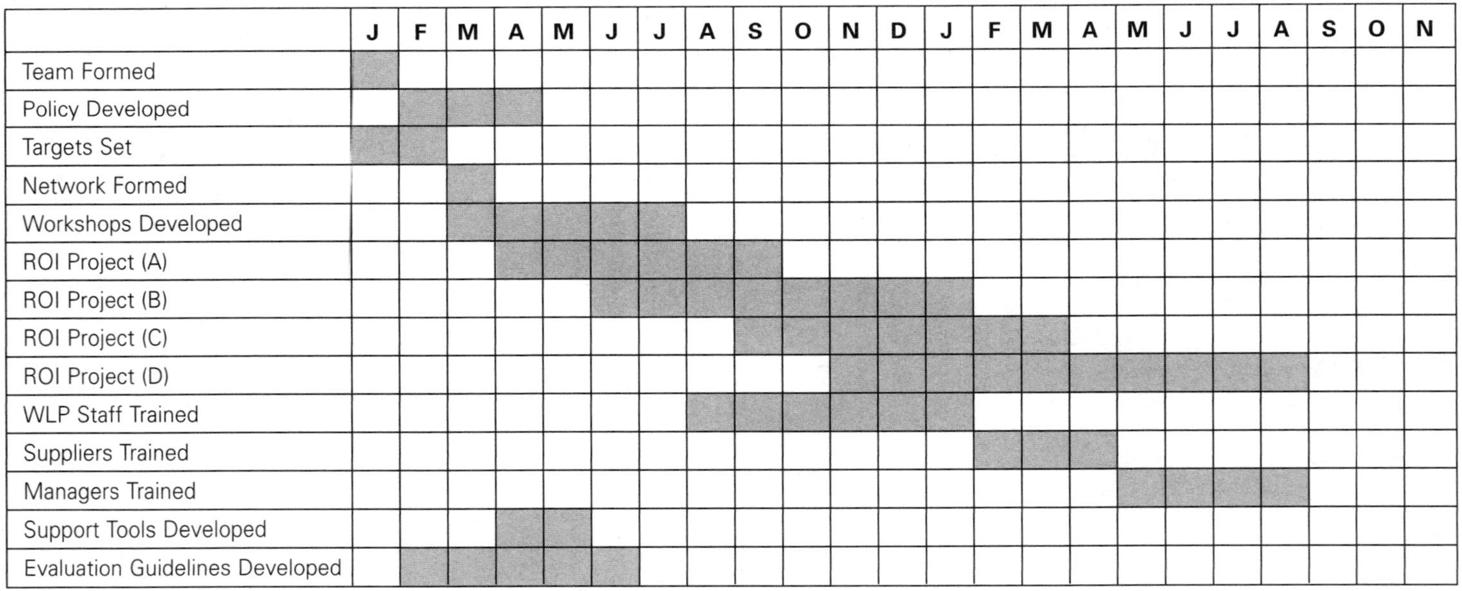

Task	J	F	M	A	M	J	J	A	S	O	N	D	J	F	M	A	M	J	J	A	S	O	N
Team Formed	■																						
Policy Developed		■	■																				
Targets Set		■																					
Network Formed			■																				
Workshops Developed			■		■	■																	
ROI Project (A)						■	■		■														
ROI Project (B)								■	■	■	■												
ROI Project (C)											■	■	■	■									
ROI Project (D)														■	■	■	■	■	■	■			
WLP Staff Trained															■	■							
Suppliers Trained																	■						
Managers Trained																	■			■			
Support Tools Developed					■																		
Evaluation Guidelines Developed						■																	

tools. Also, the entire group discusses how to remove barriers to success and focuses on suggestions and recommendations for next steps, including developing specific plans. Finally, the next steps are developed, discussed, and configured. Ultimately, these projects must be completed and the results communicated to the appropriate audiences.

Using Technology

To ensure the measurement and evaluation are efficiently and effectively administered will require the use of technology. This can range from simple, inexpensive software purchases to complete systems for managing large amounts of data. Five areas are often addressed when technology is considered in the context of measurement and evaluation.

First, the data collected for Level 1 and the self-assessments at Level 2 need to be managed efficiently using technology. Because of the high percentage of programs evaluated, technology must to be used so that data administration and integration will not consume too many resources. A variety of tools are available ranging from using scannable documents to subscription software for processing Levels 1 and 2 data on an outsource basis. This level of data requires only simple analysis.

The second area involves Level 2 data that goes beyond the self-assessment applications. Designing tests that are more objective and checking the validity and reliability of tests may require test design software, ranging from simple test construction software to detailed software for designing all types of tests, including simulations.

A third area is software for follow-up evaluations. This often involves the use of surveys, interviews, and focus group information. A variety of software packages are available to process data from surveys and questionnaires, including qualitative analysis for focus groups and interviews.

The fourth area of consideration is software for conducting detailed results studies. Some software packages are available to carry out experimental research designs, such as a control group analysis, while others are designed to automate ROI studies using questionnaires and action plans.

Finally, your organization's learning management system may provide some, if not all, of the technology needed to administer the management and evaluation processes. Many learning management system providers have built-in evaluation tools or linkages to the most common available tools to manage the data needed for Levels 1, 2, and 3, and sometimes even 4 and 5 in the analysis.

In short, technology is an important way to ease implementation. Appropriate use of technology reduces the amount of time to collect, tabulate, analyze, and report data. When time is minimized, implementation is much easier.

Sharing Information

Because the ROI methodology is new to many individuals, it is helpful to have a peer group experiencing similar issues and frustrations. Tapping into an international network, joining or creating a local network, or building an internal network are all possible ways to use the resources, ideas, and support of others.

One way to integrate the information needs of WLP practitioners for an effective ROI evaluation process is through an internal ROI network. The concept of network is simplicity itself. The idea is to bring people who are interested in ROI together throughout the organization to work under the guidance of trained ROI evaluators. Typically, advocates within the department see both the need for beginning networks and the potential of ROI evaluation to change how the department does its work. Interested network members learn by designing and executing real evaluation plans. This process generates commitment for accountability as a new way of doing business for the department.

Preparing the Management Team

Several actions can be taken with the management team to ensure that they are supporting evaluation and using the data properly. In some cases, they need to understand more about ROI and special briefings and workshops. Four specific efforts need to be considered.

First, data needs to be presented to the management team routinely so that they understand the value of WLP, particularly application, which translates directly into new skills at the workplace and business impact and often relate directly to goals and key performance indicators. The management team also needs ROI, which shows the value of learning compared to the cost. Having routine information in these areas helps them build an appreciation for the value of learning and development so that their support will increase in the future.

The second area is to get your management team more involved in the evaluation process in the various components and steps in evaluation. In addition to reviewing data, managers may be asked to help make decisions about the fate of, or adjustments in, a particular program. They may need to be involved in collecting some of the data and supporting data collection efforts. In some cases, they may be specifying what data is needed, including assisting with the up-front business alignment. There are many places where the managers' input is needed in the accountability cycle, from the initial business alignment to setting objectives to assisting with evaluation.

The third area involves ensuring that managers get full credit for improvements. Although this is a communication and reporting issue, it is critical to ensure that managers support accountability efforts in the future. All of the improvements in the workplace (which generated the ROI) should be credited to those individuals there, with the key manager being the person responsible for it. If the WLP function takes credit for the success of the program, the relationship can sour quickly. Give the praise where it is deserved and needed.

The final area is teaching or briefing managers on the ROI methodology. Managers need to understand what the methodology is about and what it can do—and not do—for them. They need to understand the resources involved in conducting creditable ROI studies, so they can help the WLP staff use this tool more selectively. To accomplish this, the organization sometimes offers a special workshop, "Manager's Role in Learning and Development," designed for these managers. Varying in duration from one-half to two days, this practical workshop shapes critical skills and changes perceptions to enhance the support of the ROI methodology. Managers leave the workshop with an improved perception of the impact of learning and a clearer understanding of their roles in the WLP process. They often have a renewed commitment to make learning work in their organization.

Making the ROI Methodology Routine

After the ROI methodology is implemented in the organization, it must be sustained; it must become routine so that it doesn't deteriorate and fade away. Making it routine requires building it into the process so that it becomes perceived as necessary, essential, and almost effortless. This section reviews the key steps designed to make it routine.

For lasting value, measurement and evaluation ROI must be perceived as routine, not a one-time event or an add-on process. It must be considered early and often in the learning and development cycle. Evaluation studies must be planned and integrated into the WLP process as early as possible. The tasks, processes, and procedures of evaluation must be as painless as possible, increasing the odds that they will be used routinely. When evaluation becomes routine, it will become an accepted and important—and sometimes required—element in the learning and development cycle.

Making Planning Routine

Intuitively, most professionals realize that planning is an important way to minimize problems, reduce resources, and stay focused on the outcome. Nowhere is this truer than when planning a comprehensive evaluation. Planning minimizes the time required later, keeps the evaluation efficient and less expensive, and helps all stakeholders to become focused on tasks and processes. It also serves to gain buy-in from key clients and make evaluation routine. Planning is essential whenever a major evaluation study is conducted. Even if the program has been operational for some time and the evaluation is suddenly requested, planning is needed to decide how to collect, process, and report data. Ideally, the evaluation plan should be in place before the program is actually developed so that the planning may actually influence the design, development, and delivery of the WLP program.

The final step is the implementation and communication of the plan for the evaluation study. This plan details the sequence of events as they should occur from the time that the evaluation plan is developed until all information has been communicated.

These planning documents can be completed in a matter of hours when the various team members and stakeholders are available to provide input. The payoff is tremendous, as planning not only makes the process more efficient and faster, but also enhances the likelihood that it will become routine.

Integrating Evaluation Into WLP Programs

One of the most effective ways to make evaluation routine is to build it into the program. This approach changes the perception of evaluation from an add-on process to one that is an integral part of the application of learning.

Built-in evaluations can be accomplished in several ways. One of the most effective is to use action plans that serve as application tools for the skills and knowledge learned in the program. The action plan is included as part of the program, and its requirement is communicated early. Appropriate agenda time is taken to explain how to develop and use the action plan and, ideally, participants are provided program time to complete it. The follow-up on success of the action plan provides data for evaluation. In this context, the action plan becomes an application tool instead of an evaluation tool. The commitment to the participants is that the completed action plan data will be summarized for the entire sample group and returned to them so that each member can see what others have accomplished. This provides a little of "what's in it for me" for the participants. Action plans are used to drive not only application and implementation data, but also business results data.

Another built-in technique is to integrate the follow-up questionnaire with the WLP program. Ample time should be provided to review the items on the questionnaire and secure a commitment to provide data. This step-by-step review of expectations helps clarify confusing issues and improves response rates as participants make a commitment to provide the data. This easy-to-accomplish step can be a powerful way to enhance data collection. It prevents the need for constant reminders to participants to provide data at a later follow-up.

Reaction and learning evaluation are usually built into the WLP program because reaction and learning measures are routinely captured. Still, application and impact data can be collected during the successive learning programs as well.

Using Shortcuts

One of the most significant barriers to the implementation of measurement and evaluation is the potential time and cost involved in implementing the process. An important tradeoff exists between the task of additional analysis versus the use of shortcut methods, including estimation. In those tradeoffs, shortcuts win almost every time. An increasing amount of research shows shortcuts and estimates, when provided by those who know a process best (experts), can be even more accurate than more sophisticated, detailed analysis. Essentially, evaluators try to avoid the high costs of increasing accuracy because it just doesn't pay off.

Sometimes, the perception of excessive time and cost is only a myth; at other times, it is a reality. Most organizations can implement the evaluation methodology for about 3% to 5% of the WLP budget. Nevertheless, evaluation still commands significant time and monetary resources. A variety of approaches have commanded much attention recently and represent an important part of the implementation strategy.

Take Shortcuts at Lower Levels. When resources are a primary concern and shortcuts need to be taken, it is best to take them at lower levels in the evaluation scheme. This is a resource allocation issue. For example, if impact evaluation (Level 4) is conducted, Levels 1 to 3 do not have to be as comprehensive. This shift places most of the emphasis on the highest level of the evaluation.

Fund Measurement and Evaluation With Program Cost Savings. Almost every ROI impact study generates data from which to make improvements. Results at different levels often show how the program can be altered or completely redesigned to make it more effective and efficient. These actions can lead to cost savings. In a few

Think About This

As a percentage of the total WLP budget, how much do you currently spend on evaluation?

cases, the program may have to be eliminated because it is not adding value and no amount of adjustment will result in program improvement. In this case, substantial cost savings can be realized as the program is eliminated. A logical argument can be made to shift a portion of these savings to fund additional measurement and evaluation. Some organizations gradually migrate to the 5% of budget target for expenditures for measurement and evaluation by using the savings generated from the use of evaluation. This provides a disciplined and conservative approach to additional funding.

Use Participants. One of the most effective cost-saving approaches is to have participants conduct major steps of the process. Participants are the primary source for understanding the degree to which learning is applied and has driven success on the job. The responsibilities for the participants should be expanded from the traditional requirement of involvement in learning activities and application of new skills. They must be asked to show the impact of those new skills and provide data about success as a routine part of the process. Consequently, the role of the participant can be expanded from learning and application to measuring the impact and communicating information.

Use Sampling. Not all programs require comprehensive evaluation, nor should all participants necessarily be evaluated in a planned follow-up. Thus, sampling can be used in two ways. First, you may select only a few programs for Levels 4 and 5 evaluation. Those programs should be selected based on the criteria described earlier in this book. Next, when a particular program is evaluated, in most cases, only a sample of participants should be evaluated to keep costs and time to a minimum.

Use Estimates. Estimates are an important part of the process. They are also the least expensive way to arrive at a number or value. Whether isolating the effects of the WLP program or converting data to monetary value, estimates can be a routine and credible part of the process. The important point is to make sure the estimate is credible and follows systematic, logical, consistent steps.

Use Internal Resources. An organization does not necessarily have to employ consultants to develop ROI studies and address other measurement and evaluation issues. Internal capability can be developed, eliminating the need to depend on consultants, which adds to the cost. This approach is perhaps one of the most significant timesavers. The difference in using internal resources versus external consultants can save as much as 50% to 60% of the costs of a specific project.

Use Standard Templates. Most organizations don't have the time and resources to customize each evaluation project. To the extent possible, develop standard instruments that can be used over and over. If customization is needed, it is only a minor part of it. For example, the reaction questionnaire should be standardized and automated to save time and to make evaluation routine. Learning measurements can be standard and built into the reaction evaluation questionnaire, unless methods that are more objective are needed, such as testing, simulation, and skill practices. Follow-up evaluation questionnaires can be standard, with only a part of the questionnaire being customized. Patterned interviews can be developed as standard processes. Focus group agendas also can be standard. Standardize as much as possible so that evaluation forms are not reinvented for each application. As a result, tabulation is faster and often less expensive. When this is accomplished, evaluation will be routine.

Use Streamlined Reporting. Reporting data can be one of the most time-consuming parts of evaluation, taking precious time away from collecting, processing, and analyzing data. Yet, reporting is often the most critical part of the process, because many audiences need a variety of information. When the audience understands the evaluation methodology, they can usually digest information in a brief format. For example, it is possible to present the results of a study using a one-page format. It is, however, essential for the audience to understand the approach to evaluation and the principles and assumptions behind the methodology; otherwise, they will not understand what the data means.

The good news is that many shortcuts can be taken to supply the data necessary for the audience and manage the process in an efficient way. All these shortcuts are important processes that can help make evaluation routine because when evaluation is expensive, time consuming, and difficult, it will never become routine.

Getting It Done

Now it is time to develop your ROI implementation plan, using the outline below. Items may be added or removed so that this becomes a customized document. This plan summarizes key issues presented in the book and will help you as you move beyond the basics of ROI.

Measurement and evaluation strategy and plan

This document addresses a variety of issues that make up the complete measurement and evaluation strategy and plan. Each of the following items should be explored and decisions made regarding the specific approach or issue.

Purposes of Evaluation

From the list of evaluation purposes, select the specific purposes relevant to your organization:

☐ Determine success in achieving program objectives.
☐ Identify strengths and weaknesses in the learning and development process.
☐ Set priorities for learning and development resources.
☐ Test the clarity and validity of tests, cases, and exercises.
☐ Identify the participants who were most (or least) successful with the program.
☐ Reinforce major points made during the program.
☐ Decide who should participate in future programs.
☐ Compare the benefits to the costs of a learning and development program.
☐ Enhance the accountability of learning and development.
☐ Assist in marketing future programs.
☐ Determine if a program was an appropriate solution.
☐ Establish a database to assist management with decision making.
   Are there any others?

_____

_____

_____

Overall Evaluation Purpose Statement

_____

_____

_____

_____

Stakeholder Groups

Identify specific stakeholders that are important to the success of measurement and evaluation.

_____

_____

Evaluation Targets and Goals

List the approximate percentage of programs currently evaluated at each level. List the number of programs you plan to evaluate at each level by a specific date.

Level	Current Use	Planned Use	Date
Reaction and Planned Action			
Learning			
Application			
Business Impact			
ROI			

Staffing

Indicate the philosophy of using internal versus external staff for evaluation work and the number of staff involved in this process part-time and full-time.

Internal versus external philosophy _____

_____

Number of staff part-time _____

Names or titles _____

_____

Number of staff full-time _____

Names or titles _____

_____

Responsibilities

Detail the responsibilities of different groups in learning and development. Generally, specialists are involved in a leadership role in evaluation, and others are involved in providing support and assistance in different phases of the process.

Group	Responsibilities

Budget

The budget for measurement and evaluation in best practice organizations is 3% to 5% of the learning and development budget. What is your current level of measurement and evaluation investment? What is your target?

_____

_____

Data Collection Methods

Indicate the current data collection methods used and planned for the different levels of evaluation.

	Current Use	Planned Use
Level 1		
Questionnaires	☐	☐
Focus groups	☐	☐
Interviews	☐	☐
Level 2		
Objective tests	☐	☐
Questionnaires/surveys	☐	☐
Simulations	☐	☐
Self-assessments	☐	☐
Level 3		
Follow-up surveys	☐	☐
Observations	☐	☐
Interviews	☐	☐
Follow-up focus groups	☐	☐
Action planning	☐	☐
Level 4		
Follow-up questionnaires	☐	☐
Action planning	☐	☐
Performance contracting	☐	☐
Performance records monitoring	☐	☐

Building Capability

How will staff members develop their measurement and evaluation capability?

Action	Audience	Who Conducts/Organizes
ROI briefings one to two hours		
Half-day ROI workshop		
One-day ROI workshop		
Two-day ROI workshop		
ROI certification		
Coaching		
ROI conferences		
Networking		

Use of Technology

How do you use technology for data collection, integration, and scorecard reporting, including technology for conducting ROI studies? How do you plan to use technology?

	Current Use	Planned Use
Surveys	☐	☐
Tests	☐	☐
Other data collection	☐	☐
Integration	☐	☐
ROI	☐	☐
Scorecards	☐	☐

Communication Methods

Indicate the specific method you currently use to communicate results. What method do you plan to use?

	Current Use	Planned Use
Meetings	☐	☐
Interim and progress reports	☐	☐
Newsletters	☐	☐
Email and electronic media	☐	☐
Brochures and pamphlets	☐	☐
Case studies	☐	☐

Use of Data

Indicate how you currently use evaluation data by placing a "✓" in the appropriate box. Indicate your planned use of evaluation data by placing an "X" in the appropriate box.

Strategy	Appropriate Level of Data				
	1	2	3	4	5
Adjust program design					
Improve program delivery					
Influence application and impact					
Enhance reinforcement for learning					
Improve management support for learning and development					
Improve satisfaction with stakeholders					
Recognize and reward participants					
Justify or enhance budget					
Develop norms and standards					
Reduce costs					
Market learning and development programs					
Expand implementation to other areas					

Questions or Comments

_____

_____

_____

_____

_____

_____

Appendix

ROI Forecasting Basics

Although beyond the scope of this book, it is important to introduce the basics of forecasting. There are a variety of forecasting techniques available. The most common are the use of preprogram forecasts, pilot programs, and Level 1 forecasts.

Preprogram Forecasts

Preprogram forecasts are ideal when you are deciding between two programs designed to solve the same problem. They also serve well when considering one very expensive program or deciding between one or more delivery mechanisms. Whatever your need for preprogram forecasting, the process is similar to postprogram ROI.

Noted

When conducting a preprogram forecast, the step of isolating the effects of the program is omitted. It is assumed that the estimated results are referring to the influence on the program under evaluation.

Figure A-1 shows the basic forecast model. As shown, an estimate of the change in results data expected to be influenced by the program is the first step in the process. From there data conversion, cost estimates, and the calculation are the same as in postprogram analysis. The anticipated intangibles are speculative in forecasting, but they can be indicators of which measures may be influenced beyond those included in the ROI calculation.

Figure A-1. Basic ROI forecasting model.

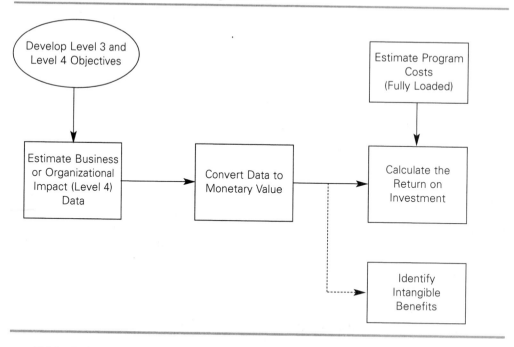

Table A-1 presents 10 steps in developing a preprogram ROI forecast.

Pilot Program

A more accurate forecast of program success is through a small scale pilot, developing ROI based on postprogram data. There are five steps to this approach:

1. As in the preprogram forecast, develop Levels 3 and 4 objectives.
2. Initiate the program on a small scale without all the bells and whistles. This keeps the cost low without sacrificing the fundamentals of the program.
3. Fully implement the program with one or more of the typical groups of individuals who can benefit from the program.
4. Develop the ROI using the ROI methodology for postprogram analysis.
5. Decide whether to implement the program throughout the organization based on the results of the pilot program.

Using a pilot postprogram evaluation as your ROI forecast will allow you to report the actual story of program success for the pilot group, reporting results at all five levels of evaluation, including intangible benefits.

Table A-1. Ten steps to forecast ROI.

1. Develop Level 3 and 4 objectives with as many specifics as possible.
2. Estimate or forecast the monthly improvement in the business impact data (ΔP).
3. Convert the business impact data to monetary values (V) using one or more of the methods described in chapter 5.
4. Develop the estimated annual impact (ΔI) in monetary terms by multiplying the monthly improvement times the value times 12: $\Delta I = \Delta P \times V \times 12$.
5. Factor additional years into the analysis if a program will have a significant useful life beyond the first year.
6. Estimate the fully loaded cost of the program (C), using the cost summary profile shown in chapter 5.
7. Calculate the forecasted ROI using the total projected benefits and the estimated cost in the standard ROI formula:

$$ROI\ (\%) = \frac{\Delta I \times C}{C} \times 100$$

8. Use sensitivity analysis to develop several potential ROI values with different levels of potential improvements.
9. Identify potential intangible benefits by obtaining input from those most knowledgeable of the situation.
10. Communicate the ROI projection and anticipated intangibles with care and caution. Remember: Although you have based the forecast on several clearly defined assumptions, there is still room for error.

Level 1 ROI

A simple approach to forecasting ROI for a new program is to add a few questions to the standard Level 1 evaluation questionnaire. As in the case of preprogram forecast, the data is not as credible as in an actual postprogram evaluation; however, a Level 1 evaluation at a minimum relies on data from participants who have actually attended the program.

Table A-2 presents a brief series of questions that can develop a forecast ROI at the end of a program. Using this series of questions, participants detail how they plan to use what they have learned and the results that they expect to achieve. They are asked to convert their anticipated accomplishments into an annual monetary value and show the basis for developing the values; they moderate their response with a confidence estimate to make the data more credible while allowing participants to reflect on their uncertainty with the process. Several adjustments are made to the data to develop the total anticipated monetary benefits. The projected costs are developed to compare with the monetary benefits to develop an ROI calculation.

Though not as reliable as actual data, this process provides some indication of potential program success.

Table A-2. Questions for Level 1 ROI.

- As a result of this program, what specific actions will you attempt as you apply what you have learned?

  _____

  _____

  _____

- Indicate what specific measures, outcomes, or projects that will change as a result of your action.

  _____

  _____

  _____

- As a result of these anticipated changes, estimate (in monetary values) the benefits to your organization over a period of one year. $_____

- What is the basis of this estimate?

  _____

  _____

  _____

- What confidence, expressed as a percentage, can you put in your estimate?
  (0% = no confidence; 100% = certainty) _____%

Additional Approaches to Forecasting

Other approaches to forecasting include the use of Level 2 test data. A reliable test, reflecting the content of WLP programs, is validated against job performance data (impact measures). With a statistically significant relationship between test scores and job performance, test scores should relate to improved job performance. The performance can be converted to monetary value and the test scores can then be used to estimate the monetary impact from the program. When compared to projected costs, the ROI is forecasted.

Another approach is Level 3 ROI. This approach places monetary value on competencies. A very simple approach to forecasting ROI using improvement with competencies is to:

1. Identify the competencies.
2. Determine the percentage of the skills that are actually applied on the job.

3. Determine the monetary value of the competencies using salary and benefits of participants.
4. Determine the increase in skill level.
5. Calculate the monetary benefits of the improvement.
6. Compare the monetary benefits to the cost of the program.

Table A-3 presents a basic example of forecasting ROI using Level 3 data.

Table A-3. Forecasting ROI at Level 3.

Ten supervisors attend a four-day learning program.

1. Identify competencies: Supervisor Skills
2. Determine percentage of skills actually used on the job: 80% (average of group)
3. Determine the monetary value of the competencies using salary and benefits of participants: $40,000 per participant

Multiply percentage of skills used on the job by the value of the job.

$$\$50,000 \times 80\% = \$40,000$$

Dollar value of the competencies for the group: $40,000 \times 10 = \$400,000$.

4. Determine increase in skill level: 10% increase (average of group)
5. Calculate the monetary benefits of the improvement: $40,000

Multiply the dollar value of the competencies by the improvement in skill level.

$$\$400,000 \times 10\% = \$40,000$$

6. Compare the monetary benefits to the cost of the program: ROI of 166%

The cost of the program is $15,000.

$$\text{ROI} = \frac{\$40,000 - \$15,000}{\$15,000} \times 100 = 166\%$$

A more comprehensive approach to Level 3 ROI is the use of utility analysis. Utility analysis should be considered when it is important to provide monetary value to behavior change.

Forecasting is an excellent tool when an actual ROI study is not feasible. A word of caution, however, if you forecast, forecast frequently. It needs to be pursued regularly to build experience and a history of use. Also, it is always helpful to conduct an actual ROI study following a forecast and compare the results to develop better skills for the forecasting process.

References

Cascio, W.F. (2000). *Costing Human Resources: The Financial Impact of Behavior in Organizations*. Australia: South-Western College Publishing.

Delcol, K., S. Wolfe, and K. West. "Can Innovation Tools Influence the New Product Development Process?" http://debonogroup.com/return-on-investment.htm (accessed July 23, 2005).

Government Accountability Office. (2003). *Human Capital: A Guide for Assessing Strategic Training and Development Efforts in the Federal Government*. GAO-03-893G.

Harris, R.L. (1999). *Information Graphics: A Comprehensive, Illustrated Reference*. New York: Oxford University Press.

Heskett, J., W. Sasser, and L. Schlesinger. (1997). *The Service Profit Chain: How Leading Companies Link Profit and Growth to Loyalty, Satisfaction, and Value*. New York: Free Press.

Horngren, C. (1982). *Cost Accounting*. Englewood Cliffs, NJ: Prentice Hall.

Howard, T. (May 16, 2005). "Brewers Get Into the Spirits of Marketing." *USA Today*.

Phillips, J.J., editor. (1997). *Measuring Return on Investment*, volume 2. Alexandria, VA: ASTD Press.

Phillips, J.J. (2000). *The Consultants Scorecard: Tracking Results and Bottom-Line Impact of Consulting Projects*. New York: McGraw-Hill.

Phillips, J.J. (2003). *Return on Investment in Training and Performance Improvement Programs*, 2nd edition. Boston: Butterworth-Heinemann.

Phillips, J.J., and P.P. Phillips. (2005). *ROI at Work*. Alexandria, VA: ASTD Press.

Phillips, J.J., R.D. Stone, and P.P. Phillips. (2001). *The Human Resources Scorecard: Measuring the Return on Investment*. Boston: Butterworth-Heinemann.

Phillips, P.P., editor. (2001). *Measuring Return on Investment*, volume 3. Alexandria, VA: ASTD Press.

Phillips, P.P., editor. (2002). *Measuring ROI in the Public Sector*. Alexandria, VA: ASTD Press.

Phillips, P.P. (2003). *Training Evaluation in the Public Sector.* Doctoral dissertation, The University of Southern Mississippi, International Development.

Prest, A.R. (1965, December). "Cost-Benefit Analysis: A Survey." *The Economic Journal.*

Sibbett, D. (1997). "Harvard Business Review: 75 Years of Management Ideas and Practices 1922-1977." *Harvard Business Review.*

Thompson, M.S. (1980). *Benefit-Cost Analysis for Program Evaluation.* Thousand Oaks, CA: Sage Publications.

Tufte, E.R. (1983). *The Visual Display of Quantitative Information.* Cheshire, CT: Graphics Press.

Wharff, D. (2005). Presentation for ADET E8 Learning Analytics and Strategies: "Serving the Enterprise."

Additional Resources

■ ■

Following are additional resources available to assist with the understanding, use, and application of the ROI methodology presented in this book.

Books on ROI

Phillips, J.J. (1997). *The Handbook of Training Evaluation and Measurement Methods*, 3rd edition. Woburn, MA: Butterworth-Heinemann.

Phillips, J.J. (2000). *The Consultant's Scorecard: Tracking Results and Bottom-Line Impact of Consulting*. New York: McGraw-Hill.

Phillips, J.J. (2005). *Investing in Your Company's Human Capital: Strategies to Avoid Spending Too Little or Too Much*. New York: AMACOM.

Phillips, J.J., and P.P. Phillips. (2005). *Proving the Value of HR: How and Why to Measure ROI*. Alexandria, VA: SHRM.

Phillips, J.J., and R.D. Stone. (2002). *How to Measure Training Results: A Practical Guide to Tracking the Six Key Indicators*. New York: McGraw-Hill.

Phillips, P.P., J.J. Phillips, R.D. Stone, and H. Burkett. (Forthcoming). *ROI Fieldbook*. Woburn, MA: Butterworth-Heinemann.

Phillips, P.P. (2002). *The Bottomline on ROI*. Atlanta, GA: CEP Press.

Case Studies Describing ROI Application

Phillips, J.J., editor. (1994). *In Action: Measuring Return on Investment* volume 1. Alexandria, VA: ASTD Press.

Phillips, J.J., editor. (1997). *In Action: Measuring Return on Investment* volume 2. Alexandria, VA: ASTD Press.

Phillips, J.J., editor. (1998). *In Action: Implementing Evaluation Systems and Processes*. Alexandria, VA: ASTD Press.

Phillips, J.J., editor. (2000). *In Action: Performance Analysis and Consulting*. Alexandria, VA: ASTD Press.

Phillips, J.J., and P.P. Phillips. (2005). *ROI at Work*. Alexandria, VA: ASTD Press.

Phillips, P.P., editor. (2001). *In Action: Measuring Return on Investment* volume 3. Alexandria, VA: ASTD Press.

Phillips, P.P., editor. (2002). *In Action: Measuring ROI in the Public Sector*. Alexandria, VA: ASTD Press.

Pope, C., and J.J. Phillips, editors. (2001). *In Action: Implementing E-learning Solutions*. Alexandria, VA: ASTD Press.

Schmidt, L., and J.J. Phillips, editors. (2003). *In Action: Implementing Training Scorecards*. Alexandria, VA: ASTD Press.

Infoline: The How-to Reference Tool for Training and Performance Professionals

The *Infoline* series from ASTD offers a variety of brief publications with tools, templates, and job aids included. The following focus on each of the five levels of evaluation discussed in this book:

ASTD. (1997). "Essentials for Evaluation." *Infoline*, 259705.

ASTD. (1998, 2000). "Level 5 Evaluation: Mastering ROI." *Infoline*, 259805.

ASTD. (1999). "Level 1 Evaluation: Reaction and Planned Action." *Infoline*, 259813.

ASTD. (1999). "Level 2 Evaluation: Learning." *Infoline*, 259814.

ASTD. (1999). "Level 3 Evaluation: Application." *Infoline*, 259815.

ASTD. (1999). "Level 4 Evaluation: Business Results." *Infoline*, 259816.

ASTD. (2001). "Managing Evaluation Shortcuts." *Infoline*, 250111.

ASTD. (2003). "Evaluation Data: Planning and Use." *Infoline*, 250304.

Books on Displaying Data

Tufte, E.R. (1990). *Envisioning Information*. Cheshire, CT: Graphics Press.

Tufte, E.R. (1997). *Visual Explanations: Images and Quantities, Evidence and Narrative*. Cheshire, CT: Graphics Press.

About the Authors

▪ ▪

Patricia Pulliam Phillips

Patti Phillips is president of The ROI Institute, the leading source of ROI competency building, implementation support, networking, and research. She is also chairman and CEO of The Chelsea Group, an international consulting organization supporting organizations and their efforts to build accountability into their training, human resources, and performance improvement programs with a primary focus of building accountability in public sector organizations. She helps organizations implement the ROI methodology in countries around the world, including South Africa, Singapore, Japan, New Zealand, Australia, Italy, Turkey, France, Germany, Canada, and the United States.

Patti's interest in accountability and evaluation began at an early age. This followed her throughout academia and 13 years in corporate life. As manager of the market planning and research organization in a large electric utility, she was responsible for the rate programs for residential and commercial customers. While in this role she played an integral part in establishing Marketing University, a learning environment that supported the needs of new sales and marketing representatives.

In 1997, Patti took advantage of an opportunity to pursue a career in a growing consulting business at which time she was introduced to the ROI methodology. Since 1997, she has embraced the ROI methodology by committing herself to ongoing research and practice. To that end, Patti has implemented ROI in private and public sector organizations. She has conducted ROI results studies on programs, such as leadership development, sales, new hire orientation, human performance improvement programs, as well as K–12 educator development, educator National

Board Certification mentoring program, and faculty fellowship programs. She is currently expanding her interest in public sector accountability through the application of the ROI methodology in community and faith-based initiatives, including Citizen Corps and AmeriCorps.

Patti's academic accomplishments include a Ph.D. in international development and a master of arts in public and private management. She is certified in ROI evaluation and has been awarded the designation of Certified Performance Technologist. She has authored a number of publications on the subject of accountability and ROI. Patti's most recent publications include *ROI at Work*; *Proving the Value of HR: How and Why to Measure ROI*; *Make Training Evaluation Work*; *The Bottomline on ROI*; *Measuring Return on Investment*, volume 3; *Measuring ROI in the Public Sector*; *Retaining Your Best Employees*; and *The Human Resources Scorecard: Measuring Return on Investment*. She has also written for the ASTD *Infoline* series, including "Planning and Using Evaluation Data," "Mastering ROI," and "Managing Evaluation Shortcuts." She is published in a variety of journals, serves as adjunct faculty teaching training evaluation, and speaks on the subject at conferences, including ASTD's International Conference and Exposition and the ISPI International Conference.

Patti Phillips can be reached at patti@roiinstitute.net.

Jack J. Phillips

As a world-renowned expert on measurement and evaluation, Jack J. Phillips is chairman of The ROI Institute. Through the Institute, Phillips provides consulting services and workshops for *Fortune* 500 companies and major organizations throughout the world. Phillips is also the author or editor of more than 30 books and 100 articles.

His expertise in measurement and evaluation is based on more than 27 years of corporate experience in five industries (aerospace, textiles, metals, construction materials, and banking). Phillips has served as training and development manager at two *Fortune* 500 firms, senior human resources officer at two firms, president of a regional federal savings bank, and management professor at a major state university.

Phillips' background in training and human resources led him to develop the ROI methodology—a revolutionary process that provides bottom-line figures and accountability for all types of training, performance improvement, human resources, and technology programs.

Books most recently authored or co-authored by Phillips include *ROI at Work*; *Investing in Your Company's Human Capital: Strategies to Avoid Spending Too Little or Too Much*; *Proving the Value of HR: How and Why to Measure ROI*; *Return on Investment in Training and Performance Improvement Programs*, 2nd edition; *How to Measure Training Results*; *The Human Resources Scorecard*; *The Consultant's Scorecard*; *Managing Employee Retention*. Phillips served as series editor for ASTD's *In Action* casebook series and serves as series editor for Butterworth-Heinemann's *Improving Human Performance* series.

Phillips has undergraduate degrees in electrical engineering, physics, and mathematics, a master's degree in decision sciences from Georgia State University, and a Ph.D. in human resource management from the University of Alabama.

Jack Phillips can be reached at jack@roiinstitute.net.